SEEN & HEARD

*America's Youngest Pundit Tackles the Lies
and the Truths of Politics and Culture*

KYLE WILLIAMS

WND BOOKS

Nashville

A Division of Thomas Nelson, Inc.

www.WNDBooks.com

Published in Nashville, Tennessee, by Thomas Nelson, Inc.

Unless otherwise noted, Scripture quotations are from the HOLY BIBLE: NEW INTERNATIONAL VERSION®. Copyright © 1973, 1978, 1984 by International Bible Society. Used by permission of Zondervan Publishing House. All rights reserved.

Scripture quotation noted NEB is from THE NEW ENGLISH BIBLE. Copyright © 1961, 1970 by The Delegates of the Oxford University Press and the Syndics of the Cambridge University Press. Reprinted by permission.

Library of Congress Cataloging-in-Publication Data

Williams, Kyle.
    Seen & heard : America's youngest pundit tackles the lies and the truths of politics and culture / Kyle Williams.
      p. cm.
    ISBN 0-7852-6368-3 (hardcover)
    1. United States—Politics and government—2001– 2. United States—Social conditions—1980– 3. Political culture—United States. 4. Popular culture—United States. I. Title: Seen and heard. II. Title.
E903.W555 2003
320.52'0973—dc21   2003002254

TO MY PARENTS,
FOR THEIR DEDICATION AND SUPPORT
THROUGHOUT MY LIFE

CONTENTS

CONTENTS

SOUND OFF: THE RIGHT CHOICE

INTRODUCTION

Slighted for Youth

Let no one slight you because you are young. (NEB)
—PAUL THE APOSTLE

THE IDEA OF HAVING YOUNGSTERS IN THE POLITICAL arena has always been debatable. Do teenagers have the ability to come up with sound opinions? Aren't the political opinions of young people simply the opinions of influential parents or mentors? Shouldn't the youth of the nation remain innocent and not become involved in the stressful world?

Getting involved as a young American is sometimes difficult and often discouraged. The United States Congress made up its mind with the campaign finance reform legislation that forbade anyone seventeen or younger from donating to a political campaign. Beyond that hindrance, I receive letters all the time telling me to go out, play football, chase girls, and forget about politics.

Then again, I receive words of encouragement constantly from readers of my WorldNetDaily column. Many organizations have been formed that encourage, promote, and organize political movements among the youth of the nation, such as the conservative Young Republican groups across the nation, Teenagers for Republican Victory, and other independent groups.

So, do teenagers have the ability to come up with sound political opinions? Yes, they do. Examples? Well, I'd like to nominate myself.

In my mind, I'd like to think that the words I am currently writing are my own opinions that I have come up with. The naysayers will complain that I am brainwashed, regurgitating the words of my parents, and might even be a diabolical poster boy for an evil right-wing news site.

Okay. That might be going too far, but take it to the edge. "A thirteen-year-old child simply does not possess the life experience, intellectual skills, or moral development to form a lasting and valid opinion about any topic," they snort.

While the argument may consist of one word against another, the validity of young opinions has much to its name. At what point can you say that an opinion is valid? Eighteen? Twenty? Twenty-five? Thirty? Do you need a college degree? Bachelor's? Master's? Doctorate? How many degrees must you have to give an intelligent opinion? At what point in time does the political view of an American become legitimate? "Chronological snobbery," as C. S. Lewis called it, is soft ground to stand on.

You see, life experience is not the same as intelligence, and lack of life experience doesn't equal ignorance. For every ignorant teenager, I can give you an ignorant American of considerable age. My old next-door neighbor voted for Bill Clinton because he looked like a nice guy—he was old enough to be considered intelligent, according to some.

This argument makes positively no sense. While, I admit, there are ignorant kids who ramble on and on about something they are clueless (on both sides of the parties), I can find the same nonsense in adult commentators and politicos, too. It works both ways. Although in this liberal-tilting landscape, being conservative might just destroy any sense of credibility!

Next, what about the charge of indoctrination or brainwashing? Rubbish. Grounding a person in the opinion of which he is raised and swaying a person from one opinion to another is not brainwashing. My *Webster's* defines *brainwashing* as "a forcible indoctrination to induce someone to give up basic political, social, or religious beliefs and attitudes and to accept contrasting regimented ideas," or "persuasion by propaganda."

Young people are just as free to reject their parents' teachings as accept them, and an organization formed and run by adults that is in existence for upcoming political generations is not brainwashing. No one is forced to join such groups, which serve a great purpose in mentoring and helping those who are interested in politics and government.

In fact, the political parties, namely, the Republicans and Libertarians, must get on the ball with such things. The left wing of politics has noticeably taken over a monopoly in the markets that are most influential to young people. Liberalism is in the entertainment industry, public education system, and the news outlets—a huge influence on society. Liberals are, undeniably, getting to kids first, and the conservatives of this nation must take notice and take action if they want to keep it.

Shouldn't the youth of the nation remain innocent and not become involved in the stressful world? No. Is that a hate-filled comment on the fringe? Definitely not.

The point is, the youth of this nation aren't innocent in the first place. Any kid that is aware of so-called entertainment is not innocent at all. You have teen "idol" Britney, who can't seem to keep her clothes on; you have MTV, which is filled with sluts left and right and an overwhelming message of sex; and then you have the Internet, which is filled with pornography traps and inappropriate junk mail messages. Not to mention the language that is used in nearly every movie that hits the wide screen and even programs on public TV.

Young people are not innocent, so don't pretend that all is well in the land of no worries in the "perfect, carefree" world.

With so many getting into the teenage years, it's about time that kids start paying attention. Before too long, my peers and I will be ruling this country, and the current leaders need to get used to the idea. After that, innocence may be restored in young people, and society might be able to dish out the right answer when asked what freedoms the First Amendment guarantees!

Back to parents and their influence: Aren't the political opinions of children just the parroting of adult influences? Not always. Young people are perfectly capable of evaluating and holding particular views. Critics say that those opinions are just built on the opinions and beliefs of other people. I partly agree. *Any political opinion that is given today is built on something else.* Nobody is that skilled at continually reinventing the wheel.

Some of the greatest books, commentaries, and other opinions have been specifically built on a person, an event, or an opinion of someone else. In addition, the views of most, even in old age, are still built on the influence of mentors and parents. It's a basic fact of life: you build on the writings of those who were before you. Remember, if you don't study history, it is bound to repeat itself.

The idea of kids giving their opinions on politics is something that should not be feared. Most times, children are not bogged down in the baggage that comes along with the usual, jaded political pundit. Allowing young people to become involved in political thought is something that can bring fresh ideas and new outlooks that are lacking in the world of punditry.

As with adult commentary, the opinion is given and presented to the readers. After that, capitalism takes over and the market rules. Therefore, if a person is spewing out nonsense concerning issues, it is dismissed and thrown away because people don't want to watch and read nonsense.

SOUNDING OFF

This book is about an inspiration; I view our nation at a crossroads in time. To have any meaning, you can have no middle ground at this time. A line has been drawn in the sand. That's what this book is about; it's about taking up arms and defending freedom.

It's about morality and the need for true education. It's about responsibility and freedom. It's about the need for a real "great" generation. If you can take a look at the writings and ideas of the age of the American Revolution, your answers are there. For abortion, homosexuality, separation of church and state, education, immorality. It's all there.

That's what I wish to focus on—responsibility. Quit depending on government, teach your children what's right, start to fight for freedom—be responsible—and most of the problems in America will be solved.

When you read this book, you'll know that it's not a plan for taking America back or a list of specific plans for success. It's more a call to arms, an attempt at inspiring, and a general battle cry for what is needed in our great nation but has been lacking too long. The United States is having a rough time, but it's not lost.

I entered this world of politics full of energy and excitement, but it's easy to become bogged down. I find myself asking, "Why couldn't my parents' generation or my grandparents' generation have just done the right thing?" Well, I have no clue why, but they didn't do the right thing. So, we're left with the problems that must be fixed, and they must be fixed now. I'm willing to give it a whirl, and I hope many other people out there will, too.

For freedom, it's worth it.

Sound Off

★ CULTURE WARS ★

1

Attacking the Family

IT'S THURSDAY NIGHT. YOU GET HOME FROM WORK exhausted, you collapse on the couch, and you turn on NBC. What do you see? Most often, it is not something a five-year-old should be exposed to, much less a teen or preteen. I don't even know how any adult could call that good, clean entertainment. This scenario could replay with almost any form of mainstream entertainment. The movies, talk shows, cable TV, public TV, or movie channels.

Many say that the entertainment part of our country is a drag on our nation and a negative influence. I have had such thoughts and even wished the entire western seaboard would fall off into the Pacific Ocean. *Adios, Hollywood!* But, of course, it's much deeper than that. Perhaps it's better to say that the entertainment industry is more of a *reflection* of America than an influence on it.

This isn't to say that all Americans are begging and pleading for the immorality that "entertainment" puts out. Moreover, many across the real America, the heartland and rural areas, despise it. It's the people who actually appreciate the immorality of American entertainment that keep it alive. But culture isn't a bunch of neatly packed, isolated boxes; it's more like a bubbling pot with everything inside roiling and rubbing up against each other. As such, the filth spills over and has a negative effect on young people and the impressionable.

I'm sure teachers ask themselves daily why their students are so disrespectful, talk in class, yell profanities, refuse to do work, and in some cases, behave violently toward their own peers and even teachers. While to avoid laying blame on uninvolved parents would be irresponsible, "entertainment" certainly does play a noticeable part in our cultural downslide.

Then again, being the greatest influence on young people, the blame for the "immoralizing" of America could be laid convincingly at the feet of the parents.

But how convincingly? Many parents allow their children to watch this sort of stuff anytime they wish. The blame could be laid at the feet of the breakdown of the nuclear family. But then why has the family broken down?

There are many factors in the destruction of the American family, but the overarching reason is an ongoing, relentless attack against the values that undergird it.

And the attack comes from all sides. Besides the hideous entertainment industry's attack on traditional Judeo-Christian values, labor unions and special-interest organizations are playing a major role in this war as well. The National Education Association (NEA), American Civil Liberties Union (ACLU), National Organization for Women, Planned Parenthood, and others continue their onslaught against these values daily.

THE ASSAULT

The NEA has made its views on homosexuality very clear in the past years, as well as revealing other aspects of its antifamily agenda. Flying under the banner of protecting youth from discrimination, groups like the NEA are indoctrinating and recruiting young Americans into the gay, lesbian, bisexual, and transgender cause.

Likewise, Planned Parenthood Federation of America plays a huge role in this war. After making sure every teen in America has a condom,

Planned Parenthood works hard to cover up the unintended results, creating a society where killing helpless children is acceptable. This organization has been and continues to be a force in public education, but has unarguably advocated an open and easy access port to abortions, condoms, and other such things for American children. Whether intentional or not, they have become a force against the family with their role in public education.

The National Organization for Women has not only supported these things, but wants any woman to have the option for abortion at any time during her pregnancy and, as a result, is partly responsible for the breakdown of the nuclear family as well.

The ACLU, clear with its agenda to take anything and everything that has to do with God out of government and based on the fallacy of separation of church and state, has worked especially hard to take God out of schools and the lives of American youth. Our nation is dripping with heritage that shows God was once important to us. God is etched into the buildings and memorials of Washington, D.C. Look at the East Coast and see how morality, justice, and American values began there—but the coast has turned into the headquarters for attacking them. Slowly, some have tried to eradicate the reminders of God in public life. It's called religious cleansing. Many of these special-interest groups, burrowing in the schools of America, recruit, teach, and indoctrinate young Americans with ideas and thoughts that no rational person would desire.

We can argue till doomsday whether the attack on the family is intentional. Of course, these organizations play dumb when faced with such accusations, but the end result is clear. Actions are actions, no matter what the thought behind them, and so is the case for this. Many of the left-wing organizations mentioned above would like people to forget what a family looks like; they don't like the picture of a mom and dad and a couple of kids.

Entertainment and left-wing organizations are continually breaking down the American family.

FORMING OPINIONS

In the world we live in, Ryan has baseball practice, Jessica has cheer practice, Mom has work, as does Dad. Obviously, many parents aren't able to watch their children all the time. Our family lives are splintered with each family member's different activities. Eating together as a family each night is almost obsolete. Sitting down to watch a movie together is extinct. Family activities are all but gone. This chaotic picture is what is now called life.

Yet, despite how it may seem, there actually used to be nuclear families. They spent their days together. They worked together; they ate together; they played together; they prayed together and went to church together. Families were strong; divorce was rare. Convictions of morality and faith had deep roots. Their way of life left little time for mischief; additionally, when discipline was needed, the consequences were stiff. Their extended family usually lived nearby or even in the same home, so they had substantial family support. Community was close-knit then; neighbors not only knew each other, but genuinely cared about each other. They had barn raisings, quilting bees, and barn dances.

We always hear this rhetoric from politicians about transforming their communities. Yet there are hardly such things as real communities in mainstream America.

A century ago, parents demanded a lot from their children. The young people were independent and had many responsibilities. Therefore, parents didn't watch them much more than many children are watched today. Bringing it back to the beginning of the chapter, what's missing in the life of 1820s Adam, as opposed to Thoroughly Modern Ryan's life, is the entertainment industry. In the 1800s rap music, video games, the Internet, movies, and all these influences were not even a speck in someone's imagination, much less invented. And that's a good thing.

Nevertheless, parents are not about to get off the hook. Along with the great moral decline of the American society, "absentee" parents are one of the big reasons. With the majority of both parents working, we find many times they seem to care more about their careers than their children. Affluence has become an enemy to many families. Instead of curled up on Mom's or Dad's lap listening to a story, little children are left in front of the television while parents are out making more money.

With involved parents, there would be no entertainment industry to speak of, much less being the way it is now.

As I talked with an acquaintance who lives abroad, I asked what is one of the things that comes to mind about America. She replied, saying that America is too liberal—not necessarily in the political sense, but in that we accept things so much more quickly and freely than other nations do, such as abortion, homosexuality, adultery, out-of-wedlock children, etc. Indeed, America does accept things quickly, rashly, and takes issues too lightly. With all the crime and corruption in the first term of the Clinton administration, he was still elected to a second term; even now that boggles the minds of many. Where have our principles gone?

Americans forget. Americans are lazy. Americans don't pay attention. It's the truth. In a sense, we are all in our little worlds where we can sit down to watch the television all day long and are not interrupted at all. Why? Because we can. The only change from that was September 11, but that was temporary. We aren't forgiving; we just forget. We rationalize evil so we don't have to deal with it. Things are hard to deal with—easier to just let them go, find diversions, or not pay attention.

Why get up from the couch, get dressed, and drive the car out to the local school to vote for the next president? Shoot! *Friends* is almost on. Who cares about voting, much less joining a political action group, attending a rally at the capitol, or reading the newspaper? The aloofness has a certain appeal to it (it caters to our innate selfishness), though it tends to be responsible for our national disasters.

SCHOOLS

Perhaps the greatest example of the effect of public schools in harming the family was at the beginning of the twentieth century. At the turn of the century, the majority of Americans were living in traditional, Christian homes and Charles Darwin's doctrine was introduced into the society, but it had very little influence and was dismissed by most.

At that time, John Dewey began his philosophy of "progressive learning"; as a signer of the Humanist Manifesto, he has been given credit for writing most of it. Included in this philosophy are attitudes that undermine the family and promote euthanasia as well as the right to abortion and divorce. Humanists, additionally, called for the undermining of parental authority.

Much of secular humanism is filled with nonsense. The Humanist Manifesto I begins:

Today man's larger understanding of the universe, his scientific achievements, and deeper appreciation of brotherhood, have created a situation which requires a new statement of the means and purposes of religion. Such a vital, fearless, and frank religion capable of furnishing adequate social goals and personal satisfactions may appear to many people as a complete break with the past. While this age does owe a vast debt to the traditional religions, it is nonetheless obvious that any religion that can hope to be a synthesizing and dynamic force for today must be shaped for the needs of this age. To establish such a religion is a major necessity of the present. It is a responsibility that rests upon this generation. We therefore affirm the following:

First: Religious humanists regard the universe as self-existing and not created. Second: Humanism believes that man is a part of nature and that he has emerged as a result of a continuous process. Third: Holding an organic view of life, humanists find that the traditional dualism of mind and body must be rejected.

The fourth affirmation runs as follows:

Humanism recognizes that man's religious culture and civilization, as clearly depicted by anthropology and history, are the product of a gradual development due to his interaction with his natural environment and with his social heritage. The individual born into a particular culture is largely molded by that culture.[1]

It goes on with more. Says the seventh affirmation, "Religion consists of those actions, purposes, and experiences which are humanly significant. Nothing human is alien to the religious. It includes labor, art, science, philosophy, love, friendship, recreation—all that is in its degree expressive of intelligently satisfying human living. The distinction between the sacred and the secular can no longer be maintained."

Again, the main writer is John Dewey, the supposed father of modern education. He shaped the teaching methods. At Columbia University, he began to teach the teachers.

As a founder of the American Association of University Professors, Dewey's philosophy began to infect the mainstream teaching of America—from elementary schools, to middle schools and high schools, to universities and colleges around the country.

In contrast to the beliefs up to twenty years before the turn of the nineteenth century, evolution began to be accepted and was later looked at as one of the greatest intellectual discoveries of the century. America turned away from God and began to seek more materialistic desires. It is no coincidence that humanists believe that there is no all-powerful God, but that we are all god over ourselves.

So, this teaching was taught, and those college students, learning from professors who completely bought into the teaching of Dewey, then went on to lead the country. Washington, D.C., and other seats of power were soon run by the "cultural elite" who knew no God but their own desires.

In an effort to reinforce the secular humanist teaching through a landmark case, the Supreme Court in 1940 found that the First Amendment required a separation of church and state. The groundwork was laid for all forms of religion and God to be removed from all public centers of learning and all areas of government.

Although it was after Dewey's time, those looking to change the culture of America took notice when the 83rd Congress's Special Committee to Investigate Tax-Exempt Foundations said, "Theoretically, a society could be completely made over in something like 15 years, the time it takes to inculcate a new culture into a rising crop of youngsters."[2]

Knowing the finding from the 1954 Special Committee, and fifteen years from the landmark Supreme Court decision, the rebellion against all forms of moral and traditional values began. Not long after that, the turbulence and sexual revolution of the 1960s began to unravel the fabric of the traditional family.

It is no surprise that the National Education Association has recognized the humanist teaching of John Dewey. NEA President Bob Chase has quoted Dewey many times in his published columns.

Adding to the already secular humanist teaching, many special-interest organizations wish to push their agenda to the young people of America in an effort to carry it out. If organizations, even as big as the National Organization for Women or Planned Parenthood, wished to lobby all fifty states in order to include certain curricula or social plans, the chances of accomplishing that are slim to none.

Enter the United States Department of Education. With the massive department all centralized to control the public schools of America, special-interest groups have an enormous ability to push their agenda to kids and teenagers.

Planned Parenthood, for instance, plans "health" days at millions of schools each year in which representatives teach homosexuality, birth control, and abortion to young people in junior high to high school, undermining the parental role in these things—frequently even running roughshod over parental teachings. Legislation in California supports programs that allow girls as young as twelve years old to have access to birth control, abortions, drug and alcohol and mental health counseling—all without any parental consent or oversight.

The education establishment becomes enemy first to parents by instilling in their children dogmas and doctrines not shared by the family, pitting one "truth" against another, and even goes so far as to seize the parental prerogative to oversee and guide their child's sexual and emotional well-being. Parents kiss good-bye their roles as teachers and counselors. Dewey's heirs have it all well in hand.

MOVIES AND TELEVISION

As I examine the entertainment industry, I wonder why this is an issue. Why are pornography sites the most visited on the Web? Why is it deemed necessary to jam-pack movies with profanities? Why, in sitcoms, are out-of-wedlock pregnancies, divorces, casual sex, and adultery all used as sources of comedy?

Hollywood is relentless with its antimarriage, antifamily message. Hollywood's view of marriage: an old-fashioned, oppressive, and frequently dangerous environment. The marriage vows are not taken seriously; divorce is the norm. Couples live together as a natural preview to marriage. Evidently, traditional families and happily married couples are out, and dysfunctional families are the popular setting.

A report by the National Fatherhood Initiative on the television dad reveals he is usually married to the mother of his children, but after that the negativism starts. The study was conducted by examining every non-sports entertainment program that aired during prime time on NBC, ABC, CBS, FOX, UPN, and the WB during March and April 2000.[3]

It reports that 25 percent of fathers on TV "are portrayed negatively." It goes on to say that when compared to the moms on the show, dads are eight times more likely to be portrayed in a negative fashion. In addition, it states that "if television wants to portray a bad parent, television almost always picks on the father."

This is particularly important in examining the war against the nuclear, American family. The head of the family is the man, who economically supports and manages the family with his wife's emotional and parental support. That's the way the traditional family has run in America, but that way is increasingly under a thundering assault.

When the figurehead of the family is denigrated in such a way, it is cause to take notice.

POLITICS AND ENTERTAINMENT

Politics and entertainment, unfortunately, go hand in hand as well. Many Americans' political beliefs are so shallow, they formulate them based on what they hear on television and in the movies.

The ironic thing about entertainment is: it is just that—entertainment. It's not real. You turn on the tube and see these "comedy" shows that have actors playing nearly every imaginable role under the sun, with witty comments followed by cussing, with a retort, and a supposedly "funny" reply. It's filled with wit, sarcasm, arrogance, and even more witty comments. If I had to live with a sitcom family, I'd go crazy. Talk about tearing down confidence and self-esteem. My mom just called me a "lamebrain, overweight geek." What do I do? Call her an "overbearing nag"? It's a world of scripts that takes entire staffs of writers to fill with "jokes."

Because politics can be made fun of so easily, it's thrown into the mix without much of an agenda. However, because the Left Coast, Hollywood crowd is filled with liberal pinkos, bias unarguably rises to the surface.

In some cases, there is an obvious political bias there for an agenda. Other times it's simply some joke. And often it could go either way. Whatever happens, the end result is that far too many people formulate their opinions on what they hear from their friends, on the radio, and on television.

Nevertheless, because entertainment is so "vital" and captivating to so many in our society, it takes priority. Who cares about the next county commission meeting or local elections when you can go to the movies and watch *South Park*?

Additionally, the public gives celebrities so much power. Many Americans actually listened to the ridiculous Alec Baldwin when he compared the 2000–2001 election with the September 11 terrorist attacks. Even Rosie O'Donnell finds it ridiculous, saying, "America gives too much credence to celebrities, to what they think and what they say."[4]

Looking at weeknight television programs, it's obvious that the antifamily situations are put in place, with out-of-wedlock pregnancies, abortions, homosexuality, and general immorality. Many say that it is not a deliberate agenda against the traditional family, but rather a market for that kind of entertainment.

Dispelling that argument, the Christian Film and Television Commission's Annual Report to Hollywood found that the more sex and nudity in a movie, the less money it rakes in. The report stated:

> Movies in 2000 with no sexual content averaged $33.8 million at the box office, more than twice as much as movies with excessive or strong sexual content. Movies in 1999 with excessive sexual content earned only $14.3 million on average, while movies with no sexual content in 1999 averaged $37.9 million.[5]

Additionally, movies with traditional and Christian values do much better at the box office in contrast to movies without. Some of the greatest movies to hit the wide screen have been good-versus-evil stories such as *The Lord of the Rings* movies, *The Fellowship of the Ring* and *The Two Towers,* and American movies such as *The Patriot* and *Men of Honor.*

Despite the fact that sex doesn't sell, movies have rampant immoral values put through under the name of "entertainment." Try going to the theaters to see a movie without sex, nudity, foul language, or other crude elements—hard, isn't it? With a war coming out of Hollywood, the immoral values in movies are rampant—with almost a deliberate agenda. Critics say that it's not a real deliberate agenda against the traditional family or values, but a huge market for that type of entertainment, yet the box-office dollars say no.

It's difficult these days to go to the movie theater to find a movie worth seeing. Not just that, but finding a movie I as a fourteen-year-old can see is challenging; sometimes the only things playing are rated R.

A study published in the journal *Effective Clinical Practice* found children in fifth grade through eighth grade who were permitted to watch R-rated movies were three times more likely to smoke cigarettes and consume alcohol than those children who were not permitted to watch R-rated movies. The results did not take into account how strict the parents were concerning other things, but one of the strongest findings of the study was the correlation between watching R-rated movies and the percentage of children consuming alcohol.[6]

Certainly, this does not prove that watching R-rated movies causes children to drink alcohol, but it does imply that viewing "adult" material where adults act irresponsibly may cause children to act the same way. This does not mean that it will directly change the way kids think, but it gives them good reason to act differently. After viewing a movie with an excess of profanity, it gets stuck in my mind but does not necessarily change the way I act.

An Associated Press survey in 1989 indicated an overwhelming majority of Americans want less violence in movies—a whopping 82 percent. Seventy-two percent said they wanted less sexual content, and another 80 percent desired less foul language in the movies.[7] Can attitudes have changed that much in a decade? If they have, one could easily argue it is only a sign that the constant antifamily erosion has taken its toll on American values.

If you ever pay attention to the recent movies, you also see, many times, homosexuality portrayed in a positive light. The essence of homosexuality is in deep contradiction with traditional family values—

the values that gave birth to America. Judeo-Christian values are foundational to American thought and life. Those Judeo-Christian values are what drove the Founders to create a world where all men were allowed to worship God freely without the fear of grave consequences.

Through the faiths of Christianity and Judaism, the values created a society where, as a rule, the family had one mother and one father—the most stable family structure—and sex was only approvingly practiced within the bounds of marriage. This was the ideal way of life during the founding of America, but it is deteriorating.

When you continually hear a certain statement over and over again, the natural reaction is to believe it, and if you say something continually, in your mind it becomes truth or, at least, becomes comfortable. With the constant stream of antifamily entertainment, how easy is it to begin denigrating and disliking what was so foundational to our nation? Too easy.

MAGAZINES AND PRINT MEDIA

Magazines geared to teens are popular and becoming more popular than ever. Although many magazines are technically geared toward those in their late teens to early twenties, the advertising and readership base contradicts this. Many teens in junior high and senior high—from twelve to eighteen—are reading the magazines that promote homosexuality, sex, dating, and many other things that wouldn't be approved of by involved parents.

Going past the half-dressed guys and girls, there are many things children are reading that their parents are not aware of.

In *Seventeen*, for instance, they have so-called experts telling you or your children that "having sex has become the equivalent of getting a driver's license. It's a rite of passage."[8]

Going further, in the magazine *Teen People*, movie and TV stars are interviewed. In one issue, actor Alyson Hannigan is interviewed; she starts out telling readers to deal with their problems instead of using drugs.[9] However, the interview quickly deteriorates, telling teens that sixteen is an acceptable age to have sex, saying, "You can drive a car. You know what's going on." Although she plays a lesbian on television and starred in the movie *American Pie*, she is considered a role model for many young teens.

Many say the statements and opinions in these magazines are harmless, and just because a person sees something that says sex is okay doesn't mean he will go out and have sex. However, they are missing the point. When a teen reads opinions and quotes from favorite actors who state, "Sex before marriage is okay," "Homosexuality is not a bad thing," he or she certainly won't have sex because she reads that, but it can influence an acceptance in the teen's mind. If one hears the same thing repeatedly, he or she is more likely to come to believe it as truth. Therefore, when the time comes, they will convince themselves with this evidence that sex before marriage is "okay," that homosexuality is "okay," that profanity is "okay."

It's an attempt to rationalize actions. You hear things here and there that you can use to justify something you know is wrong.

TURNING THE TIDE

While the life of a teen in the twenty-first century is incomparable to the life of a teen two hundred years before, it is understood that young Americans are going through a change.

People who have a core set of beliefs instilled by their parents or mentors will keep those beliefs for the remainder of their lives and immediately dispel the negative opinions from the movies, television, or magazines, preventing them from being, for lack of a better word, *brainwashed* by hearing the worldly opinions repeatedly.

Unfortunately, many parents or guardians are not involved with their child. Therein lies the biggest problem.

It goes without saying that if a parent is involved, that adult loves his or her child. But by the lack of parental involvement, what are we to conclude? The lack of parental involvement puts children in a place where they learn more about life from strangers and people who often don't share their parents' ideas about what they should be learning. It also tends to put kids under the watchful eye of the one-eyed baby-sitter, the television. Unfortunately for many young people who are my friends and peers, many parents do not care. I can see that every day by just talking to them.

These children are at a disadvantage compared to their peers who are in the safety and security of two loving parents. Children living in single-parent homes are more likely to live in poverty, be less successful in school, and be undisciplined and disrespectful. If the mother has a live-in boyfriend, child abuse is an even greater possibility than for their counterparts in loving two-parent families.

These problems do not have a quick fix, but the solution is easy to see. As with many of the problems facing America, you can simply go back to the founding of this nation to see what must be done. The overall plan of America was brilliant, but the key to its success is responsibility. Responsibility in justice, responsibility in the family, and responsibility in everything you do.

Yes, the American experiment is failing because Americans are irresponsible. It's the most apparent aspect of our culture. As I said before, we are lazy. Guys like to lie on the couch all day watching football. It's an escape from reality. The truth hurts, and it's demanding. So, just forget about it and run away. Lying on the couch playing video games sounds more relaxing than weighing the evils of entertainment, doesn't it? That's what has led us down this road.

The solution to the problem is simple: become responsible. To borrow a phrase from the liberal politicians, don't do it for yourself, but do it for the children. No, a government program won't fix it.

Up until the industrial revolution, Americans were isolated. You had your family-inherited house, with the garden and the livestock, and the small town several miles away. There was no communication. Sounds like a pretty rough time in comparison to the twenty-first century.

However, that isolation is what made America what America is. It allowed families to keep their values without temptation from outsiders. It was this way during colonial times. They didn't want to become politically involved, but they did because it was needed.

They were so firm on their principles, they risked torture and death to create a better environment for their children and generations after them. That's what we here in the twenty-first century need to do. Although no one will be facing torture or death, outside influences will always be a factor. Against the various threats, family values must be guarded. It was never the government's role to shape opinions. It was the family's.

All evidence suggests a growing trend of a return to the traditional landscape of the family. With more and more moms staying home, the growing base of homeschooling, and families moving to rural areas, it leaves us with hope.

Yes, it's possible to return to the real America. No, it will not be easy. It will take a while, but there is great reason to have hope.

The family will continue to deteriorate until mothers and fathers love each other more than themselves. Doing this gives your children a sense of security. Start doing what is best for your children. Let kids know who's the boss. They need discipline: start when they are small, be involved, talk with your children, really know them, what their strengths and weaknesses are, teach them to love, teach them to be respectful, teach them cause and effect, help them find a place to fit in, whether it be sports, music, dance, or what they enjoy doing, listen to them.

This is what you can do: put character as a higher priority than convenience. After that, instill such values in future generations. This may sound like a hopeless way to make change, but results show otherwise.

Homeschooling is relatively new but has grown over very few years. It's the same concept that trends can change in a short period of time. Parents teach their children these values and the required education they need. In turn, the children homeschool their children, and so on and so forth. Although most homeschool lines are only in their second generation, they have turned out to be extremely successful and are growing in popularity.

Responsibility is the key to success.

FURTHER READING

Books

- William J. Bennett, *The Broken Hearth: Reversing the Moral Collapse of the American Family* (New York: Doubleday, 2001).
- William J. Bennett, *The Death of Outrage: Bill Clinton and the Assault on American Ideals* (New York: Simon & Schuster, 1998).
- James C. Dobson, *Bringing Up Boys* (Wheaton, IL: Tyndale, 2001).
- Maggie Gallagher, *The Abolition of Marriage* (Washington, DC: Regnery, 1996).
- Michael Medved, *Hollywood vs. America* (New York: HarperCollins, 1992).
- James Robison, *The Absolutes: Freedom's Only Hope* (Wheaton, IL: Tyndale, 2002).
- Edith Schaeffer, *What Is a Family?* (Old Tappan, NJ: Revell, 1975).

Web Sites

- www.afa.net
- www.focusonthefamily.org
- www.citizenlink.org
- www.traditionalvalues.org

2

Intolerance to the Extreme

INTOLERANCE IS A TOPIC THAT IS ALIVE AND WELL IN American politics today. Not a day goes by that I don't hear someone demanding tolerance for something, whether it be the National Education Association, which champions the ideas of "diversity" and "multiculturalism," or other left-wing organizations such as the American Civil Liberties Union, which sponsors the ideals of communism and anti-Americanism.

This intolerance is really a matter of interpretation. For me, it's always good to be intolerant of the ideas and values that go against your beliefs. *Tolerance* has become a term to hide behind for those who are politically wishy-washy and really have no foundation.

Still, being intolerant of some things can be negative. There are some, for example, who will not compromise, will not sacrifice, and will not moderate on any issue whatsoever. To them, bipartisanship is a sin, and working together is not possible. Those are people such as Jesse Jackson, Al Sharpton, and Kim Gandy, who create much more friction than advancement.

Yet when it comes down to the wire, tolerance and intolerance are used for good and logical reasons as well as bad—such as tools for propaganda. Therefore, most times, "tolerance" is touted for demagoguery, mainly by the Left, along with all the rhetoric of "diversity," "inclusiveness," and "equality." They are not principles so much as shibboleths; stray from the path and pay the price.

The sort of intolerance that I speak of is mostly called political correctness, but it is more accurately described as a form of social oppression, a speech code, and policing of thought. It's an attempt to silence opposition and demonize traditional values, and it really comes down to a propaganda war. "Go away; you're getting in the way of diversity!" they shout, without thinking about what they just said. Nevertheless, the Left doesn't really appeal to equity or reason; it's all about a war of words and perceptions.

One example would be the NEA. They are ingenious in their public relations campaign by painting a picture of the opposition. In the 2001 NEA Resolutions, Section B-31 says,

> National Education Association believes that multiculturalism is the process of valuing differences and incorporating the values identified into behavior for the goal of achieving the common good. Multicultural education should promote the recognition of individual and group differences and similarities in order to reduce racism, homophobia, ethnic and all other forms of prejudice and to develop self-esteem as well as respect for others.[1]

Sixty-three words, and they state nothing. You read this statement and gain nothing whatsoever. What on earth does this mean? In real terms, it means that they put a pretty name on an idea that will give them power to influence my peers, my friends, maybe you, or quite possibly your children.

It gives credence to "health" workshops that teach moral equality between homosexuality and heterosexuality and allows for some schools to betray you and encourage students to "try it out." As to reducing ethnic, racist, and all forms of prejudice, it also leaves you with a million questions, but it all comes down to the fact that they are influencing the youth of the nation by making them think in "approved" ways.

It's not the job of schools to set an agenda of influence upon unsuspecting and susceptible children. It's not the job of public education to mess with the morality of a teen. And it's not the job of some special-interest union in Washington to affect the opinions of young people. Their job is to teach the "three R's": reading, writing, and arithmetic.

Yet if you dare to say such things against the power of liberal organizations, they come right back at you by saying you are racist, homophobic, and prejudiced. You might even promote "hatred in the hallways." Oh, the horror! You can't defend yourself against lies and such propaganda. That's where they win. But you ignore the lies, and then the perception of the average Joe becomes reality in his mind.

DIVISIVENESS

One effect of this so-called political correction and propaganda is divisiveness through such things as class warfare, race categories, division of experience, the scare tactics against the elderly, and then using phony victimhood in order to push an agenda.

While you could go on and on about the slander that occurs in American politics, this list of tactics is most often seen on political and moral issues. Moreover, they shine the spotlight on a need for grassroots organizations to take a handle on issues and seek to expose the lies and distortions.

This is not to say that the lies and distortions only come from the left side of the spectrum. From what I have observed on a national level, Republicans and Democrats are alike in that they both seek power. In doing that, they compromise on liberty, core beliefs, and the morality that should be seen in elected officials. Of course, in saying that, I should be clear that I believe most of the rancor and shiftiness comes from the left side of politics. This is what makes politics dirty, it's what makes politics repulsive, and it requires a sense of skepticism that all too many people don't have or don't want to have.

CLASS WARFARE

Class warfare has been in the Democratic playbook for a very long time. It's that form of propaganda that gets everyone fired up, but is based on a hatred of the so-called wealthy. Its roots are jealousy and envy.

This is most often seen in broad economic issues but mainly on tax cuts and government handouts. For a relevant example, I submit to you an ad from the 2002 Oklahoma Senate race between Republican incumbent James Inhofe and Democratic challenger David Walters.

To give you a little background, in 2001, the Senate passed the much-needed and supported economic stimulus package that boosted the economy by giving a $1.35 trillion tax break to the American people.

Back to autumn 2002: the David Walters ad opens up with sad music in the background and photos of little children playing: "They are the faces of Oklahoma's future, but one out of every five kids has no health insurance and Oklahoma ranks 43rd of 50 states in providing health care to kids who need it. Jim Inhofe could have made a difference for those kids." It continues, "Instead Inhofe turned his back on them by voting to fund tax cuts for Enron executives instead of health care coverage for the kids who need it most. Jim Inhofe. If our kids can't count on him, how can we?"

That's nice. It flows. It runs together. It may even be sad. But it paints a picture of reality that is totally false.

The perception is this: Oklahoma is in a health care crisis that is harming the state, but most important, the children. Oh, the helpless, poor, and innocent children! When they're obviously in trouble, we always call on those elected officials to take care of the problem. Instead of helping, however, the Republicans in Congress, most importantly, Jim Inhofe, have supported a tax break for wealthy big businesses, notably Enron—the people who stole millions from employees and investors, only to buy beachfront mansions while the little guy is out of a job.

This is all attempting to make a reality in which Jim Inhofe, a minion of the devil, has priorities in favor of rich, greedy hogs, instead of the poor, helpless children who need health care coverage.

The reality is this: Jim Inhofe has voted for and supported a $1.35 trillion tax break for all Americans. Instead of hiking taxes for the government to get involved, he supported a tax break that would give money to the people and then allow them to decide what to do with it. Although the government could set up a state health care program, all the money would be managed by inefficient and aloof bureaucrats, and taxes would go straight up (not to mention the unconstitutionality of it).

Last, while the effectiveness of such ads varies, it is meant to be an example of an often used, general attack that uses perception and spin to create views in the mind of the average, apolitical Joe Smith.

RACISM

Much like class, race categories are frequently used as propaganda tools by groups like the National Association for the Advancement of Colored People (NAACP) and Jesse Jackson's group, the Rainbow/ PUSH Coalition.

These categories force people of different races into certain economic, business, and importance statuses. Ironically, the people who enforce such propaganda are from organizations that claim to fight for desegregation and the rights of black people. These "special-interest" groups have forced the separation of blacks and whites—at least perceptionally—so that whites are the wealthy, suburban businessmen in suits and blacks are part of an inner-city, low-income clique that cannot merge or mingle with others. Those of other races and ethnicities are somewhat caught in between.

From the Clarence Thomas fiasco to the "Reverend" Jesse Jackson supporting high school rioters in Michigan and the O. J. Simpson trial debacle to black-on-black racism against conservative voices in

America—it all shows that being "black" has little to do with your skin color. Remember, Bill Clinton was lauded as the first black president by some in the African-American community—a distinction borne more of politics than pigment.

An example of this would be the slanderous statements made against Secretary of State Colin Powell by celebrity singer Harry Belafonte on a talk radio program in San Diego, California, in autumn 2002. As first reported nationally by the *Drudge Report*, "Belafonte . . . told host Ted Lightner that Powell was like a plantation slave who moves into the slave owner's house and only says what his master wants him to say."[2]

"There's an old saying," Belafonte said. "In the days of slavery, there were those slaves who lived on the plantation and there were those slaves that lived in the house. You got the privilege of living in the house if you served the master . . . exactly the way the master intended to have you serve him." The singer continued, "Colin Powell's committed to come into the house of the master. When Colin Powell dares to suggest something other than what the master wants to hear, he will be turned back out to pasture."

This obviously is a bash against the Republican White House and an example of how races are divided into certain categories. These divisions create a form of in-house racism that dictates certain thought patterns, assumptions, and behaviors that all must be complied with, or we are "sellouts" to our race. This makes our tint just an outside sign of inside realities of life and thought. *It's the very essence of racism, forcing a judgment based on complexion and hue, not character and how we live.*

It wasn't long after Belafonte's tirade that "Reverend" Jesse Jackson joined in with the singer, slamming Colin Powell for selling out the black race. "[Powell's] not on our team. If he wins, Trent Lott wins," Jackson told an Athens, Georgia, church in the worst sort of election politicking (the 2002 election was only days away). "We're not on that team. If he wins, we lose. If he wins, poor folks lose."[3]

Memo to people of the black race: Jesse Jackson just called *all* blacks "poor." That kind of chatter is more insulting than inclusive. Where is the outrage? Where are the protests? There are none. Remarks like Jackson's are nothing but a push to put blacks into victimhood in an effort to force an agenda that will ultimately lead African-Americans down a road of destruction.

A PH.D. IS NEEDED TO HAVE AN OPINION?

Another way of silencing political opposition is by throwing in the experience card. A campaign that has shut up many people from commenting on things such as war, the environment, the ongoing Middle East conflict, and when and where it's okay to drill for oil. Being a weekly columnist for WorldNetDaily, I have firsthand experience with this. The most recent example was the debate on attacking Iraq and Saddam Hussein in the war on terrorism.

While attacking the Taliban and terrorist clans in Afghanistan had overwhelming support right after the September 11 attacks, attacking Iraq has had less support. When I wrote my WND column, advising we attack Iraq as soon as possible, I was inundated with e-mails from those who were obviously against the attack. Among the profanities, the demands for me to join the military, and some support, most of the criticism I received played off my age and supposed lack of education and/or experience.

Yes, it's true. I confess, I have no personal experience in invading hostile Middle East nations—but then, most don't. The substitute for experience is knowledge. I can investigate the issue, study history, and make rational conclusions. But people play fast and loose here as well. It's as if you need a college degree to have an opinion. But if the content and quality of our education qualify our opinions, then it would be nearly impossible for most graduates coming out of government schools to have a legitimate opinion in politics.

Maybe the most obvious debate in which this plays is abortion. When males attack the murderous campaign of abortions in the

United States, they are thrown the experience card as well. I have written about abortion in WorldNetDaily and received comments such as, "I noticed most anti-abortionists are men; they are biologically incapable to conceive the emotional anguish a woman must suffer to come to that decision." As if the merits of the decision hinged on how hard it is to make it. Rather, the merits hinge on the result—a life is taken, something both women and men can deal with on the same level, which is perhaps why polls released by the major news organizations show that the number of males and females who identify themselves as "pro-life" are at nearly the same percentage.[4]

Another attack on experience relates to the issue of the conflict between Israel and the Arab world. Granted, it is a very complex struggle that has been going on for many, many years. Yet unless you are an elitist pinhead who believes you need a Ph.D. in every degree on the planet and must have years of experience in such an issue, it's not impossible to understand and have a firm, sensible opinion on the issue. Experience is not equal to intelligence, and wisdom doesn't always come with experience and age.

SCARE TACTICS

One very effective form of propaganda in the uncivilized world of politics is scare tactics, primarily used against the elderly and "seasoned citizens." Again, this is most often used as a tool by the left side of the political spectrum in America in order to achieve political gain through lies and distortion.

In the recent political war of the 2002 elections, the Democrats couldn't pass up the opportunity to use this tactic against the Republicans. An agenda set forth by many conservatives was the idea to allow stock market options for Social Security recipients. In a proposed program, the recipient would have full control of where the money goes, and the percentage of money to invest would be extremely slim.

Yet the Dems blasted conservatives in campaign ads, saying that they wanted to take money from seniors to put into the stock market. A "risky scheme," many blasted. Then House Minority Leader Dick Gephardt (D-MO) wailed, "The Republican House majority has produced a budget that raided $1.8 billion from the Social Security trust fund. You'll have to cut benefits for today's seniors."[5] The issue is always packaged in such a way as to freak out the elderly as much as possible.

The politics is easy enough to understand—even if it is crass and manipulative. Many of America's older citizens depend on Social Security and Medicare to keep up their way of life, but many of them don't want to spend the time playing the political games and wading through the lies. So, the Democrats sought to capitalize on that. In election 1994, when Republican Jeb Bush and Democrat Lawton Chiles were running for the governorship of Florida, Democrats called up nearly 700,000 Florida seniors living in Republican counties and proceeded to tell them that Jeb Bush would do away with Medicare if he was elected—a total falsehood but a powerful motivator to vote Democrat.

Moving ahead eight years to the elections of 2002, the Democrats again used a high-profile scare tactic for the elderly against the Republicans. A cartoon titled "Social Insecurity," sent through e-mail to thousands of people by the Democratic National Committee, illuminates a below-the-belt move.

The cartoon opens up with a young man on a beach dreaming about his retirement. Then he is shown in a wheelchair as President George Bush pushes him down a graph that is depicted as the economic downslide, and the cartoon President Bush says, "Hey, you wanna go for a ride with me? It's a risky plan, but, but trust me."

This again is blasting the Republicans on their plan to allow minimal stock options in Social Security. Later, the Republican National Committee demanded the Democrats remove and apologize for the ad, but received a response saying, "We'll apologize for the ad if they apologize for trying to deceive seniors and cheat them out of their retirement savings."[6]

There is an entire enormous age-group that depends on Social

Security and Medicare to make ends meet and provide health care. So when those people are told repeatedly that Social Security and Medicare are going to crash, burn, and die because of Republicans, it becomes an influence, no matter how absurd it is.

In response to the allegations made in the DNC cartoon, 60 Plus Association President Jim Martin stated, "Have they no shame? This is sick, in fact, sickening. To imply that President Bush or anybody else will send old folks in wheelchairs to the poor house by harming Social Security is not only deceitful but it's totally dishonest. For 40 years, first as a reporter covering Congress, and now lobbying for seniors, I have never seen such sheer hypocrisy."[7]

The group 60 Plus is seen as the conservative alternative to the American Association of Retired People and has sought to expose the lies of liberal scare tactics. Still, propaganda is difficult to defeat and only destroyed through the tough route of communication and getting the word out—a force that is needed in American politics today.

VICTIMHOOD

Merriam-Webster's Collegiate Dictionary defines *victim* as "one that is subjected to oppression, hardship, or mistreatment."

In the story of the good Samaritan, the man who stopped to take care of the wounded man on the roadside did so knowing he needed the help, because he was a victim of one thing or another. This is the way it should work: people in need get help. Since people generally agree on that point, it is a simple step to twist the desire to help victims to political advantage by creating the image of victimhood whether it exists or not.

The National Education Association has come out saying that maybe 5 percent of American students in public education could be homosexuals and may be discriminated against by other classmates.[8] What do you do next? The group has created resolutions and fought for programs that teach homosexuality in public schools. What is the reasoning behind it? By successfully painting a picture of 5 percent of public school students being mistreated, however dubious that figure may be, the NEA creates an image of victims in need of help, which allows it to push its agenda.

This tactic has been even more heavily exploited among racial minorities. The NAACP, Al Sharpton, Jesse Jackson, and many of the so-called black representatives or leaders have done the same thing against blacks.

The feminists also use victimization as a means to carry out their agenda. However inscrutable and ironic, women are portrayed as victims across the board. I've always found it interesting that women are a "minority," even though they seem to be larger in number than any other majority on the earth. Yet they still "need" help—not psychological help but political help, if that makes any sense.

This appears to be obvious in the case where CBS's *60 Minutes* played a segment on girls consistently scoring higher on subjects across the board in public education. The reason? Too much attention has been spent on girls, while boys are left out.[9] The National Organization for Women didn't like that report too much, as you may have expected. Instead of applauding the efforts in this success story of girls making a better grade in schools, NOW blasted CBS News in an action alert on October 25, 2002.[10] Why? It's obvious that if you can generate pity, a political agenda will be more readily accepted. Long-term empowerment and real advancement for women matter less than exploiting their perceived injustices in the here and now.

NOW asked readers to contact CBS News executives to demand equal time on another follow-up segment. Although I wonder why boys don't get equal attention.

NAME-CALLING

When all else fails, demagogues and propagandists can just (what else?) call people names. It's done by the Democrats and Republicans every day. It inhibits discussion, it closes off debate, it's basically indefensible, and it works!

For the homosexual community, when someone challenges or

criticizes the motives and agendas of "gay" groups, the response is almost always a personal attack. To them, there is no differentiation between someone who hates homosexuality and someone who hates homosexuals. Those who are against the homosexual movement in America are called "homophobes," "hate-mongers," "bigots," "religious wackos," "gay bashers," and then—sin of all sins—they dare to call us "intolerant." Gasp! Such was the case for Dr. Laura Schlessinger when her newly begun television program at Paramount was protested by the homosexual community. After successfully being painted as the Queen of Intolerance, her show was canceled.

Likewise, conservative blacks, such as J. C. Watts, Larry Elder, Walter E. Williams, and Thomas Sowell, are called "Oreos," "Uncle Toms," "Judases," "sellouts," "antiblack," and worse. All those who get out of ideological line are sure to get bludgeoned with slurs and character defamation.

The list continues to Judeo-Christian conservatives. I have been called a "right-wing fanatic," "religious radical," "homophobe," "small-minded," "prejudiced," "racist," and the list goes on and on.

Those who oppose any education "reform" and legislation hate children, those who oppose the school lunch program want starving kids, especially black kids, to go unfed, and those who push for education deregulation and reducing school administration size want schools to close and children to go uneducated.

If a white thirty-five-year-old American male spoke up against the National Organization for Women's agenda, that man would probably be ripped to shreds with personal attacks. However, there would be no regard at all about his arguments, just an emotional response of name-calling and propaganda.

In order to circumvent the opposition's game plan, liberals emotionally stand up and personally attack him or her and throw the person's argument out the window—it works. Thus, for a member of the majority it is very unpopular to attack the politics and policies of a race, sex, or sexual "orientation" that is considered in the minority.

Organizations such as the NAACP, NOW, NEA, Planned Parenthood, and the Rainbow/PUSH Coalition would rather you never have been able to speak at all than offer debate and discussion. Why? Because they obviously have some sort of agenda to hide. Why would they wish to hide their agenda? Apparently, it seeks to harm other people or produce other unsavory results.

Through a phony set of guidelines—more popularly known as political correctness—these personal attacks and silencing of opponents, most left-wing groups are successfully illuminating the premise of their stances. But perhaps more important, they are making their opponents look bad. Doing that gives them a great advantage in silencing their opponents. Just the possibility that a group can make a certain person look mean is enough to scare almost any politician. In a shallow climate where names and hasty judgments stick like glue, image is everything.

In 1996, I was seven years old, heading over to my neighbor's house to see his opinion on the presidential election. I didn't know much about specifics of what was going on then, but I knew that Bill Clinton was a sleazeball. Naturally, I thought my neighbor believed the same thing. However, I'll never forget when my liberal next-door neighbor told me that he was voting for Clinton because he looked like a "nice guy," and Bob Dole looked like "a mean, old man." Anytime a candidate can be sold based mainly on charisma, then politics is susceptible to manipulation by image shapers and propagandists.

Elections are decided by people like my old neighbor—those who watch the evening news long enough to hear a little blurb about a few political topics and vote for the good-looking guy.

AVERAGE AMERICANS

For anyone, especially a younger American, the social aspect of life is nearly essential. While some obviously prefer to keep to themselves, socializing is a necessity of life.

Many wonder why politics has seemingly evaded, for the most part, the area of social conversations. Although my older brother believes it is because the subject of politics is more boring than anything, the argument appears to be flawed. If politics is boring to the majority of Americans, then Web sites, newspapers, and television programs wouldn't be saturated with it. Moreover, if politics is so boring, there wouldn't be thousands of political pundits with millions of readers, viewers, and listeners.

Analysis suggests that the main reason politics escapes from the social landscape is that many people take everything personally. If you were to attack the public education system in a conversation with a mother who has had her children in public schools forever, that mother would be less than intrigued.

Furthermore, the speech code has seeped into the way mainstream Americans think. If I, for example, were to attack the actions and agendas of the leaders of the "black civil rights movement"—Jesse Jackson, Al Sharpton, etc.—there would be no differentiation, by many, between the attack on the actions of Jesse Jackson and civil rights for blacks.

This gives the Left a great advantage. Anyone who analyzes politics knows that Liberal-Democrat actions and agendas are based primarily on emotion. That emotion has made its way into the political debates of America. Besides circumventing intelligent conversations and the furthering of this country's progress through politics, it quiets those who oppose.

Because supposedly serious and mature political discussions have degraded into immature and childish behavior, it has created a resistance to the embracing of political participation. No one wants to be insulted and painted as a racist, bigot, sexist, homophobe, or radical zealot.

THE MORAL DECLINE: TOLERANCE

Perhaps the greatest reason morality across the country has hit nearly rock bottom is because of the supposed universal virtue, tolerance.

But looked at differently, one could argue that intolerance is actually a greater virtue. The intolerance that is brought up on the political battlefront is always referring to core issues—such as abortion, homosexuality, education, gun control, etc. These core beliefs are held dear to almost anyone in this country. They are molded and shaped when young and held close and rarely modified throughout life. The same issues for which many liberals are demanding tolerance are the same core issues on which one does not waver.

Many want you and me to become tolerant of homosexuality; I believe homosexuality is evil and a sin. Politically, groups want you and me to be tolerant of abortion; I believe abortion is evil and murder. And they want you and me to be tolerant of evolution and humanism taught through public education—but evolution and secular humanism contradict everything I believe in and stand for in this world.

The demand for tolerance on these issues is totally unreasonable. Segments of society must agree to disagree on certain things, but we will not become tolerant of each other's agendas actually being carried out—if so, all we have done is water down our beliefs. This might be a desired end for some; people without principles are easy to lead and manipulate—just use the right bait and gimmicks. Anyone should be able to see if that is where tolerance leads, then it is more vice than virtue.

FURTHER READING

Books

- Tammy Bruce, *The New Thought Police: Inside the Left's Assault on Free Speech and Free Minds* (Roseville, CA: Prima Publishing, 2001).

- Linda Chavez, *An Unlikely Conservative* (New York: Basic Books, 2002).

- Dinesh D'Souza, *Illiberal Education* (New York: Free Press, 1991).

- Larry Elder, *The Ten Things You Can't Say in America* (New York: St. Martin's Griffin, 2000).
- J. C. Watts, *What Color Is a Conservative* (New York: Harper Collins, 2002).

3

Media Bias

THE NEED FOR A FREE PRESS IS TREMENDOUS. NOT ONLY to prevent government propaganda, but also to prevent the views of a small group to force-feed a society with its political agenda.

The fact is that without a free press, freedom of expression and thought is all but destroyed. Without it, political activism is gone, expression of free opinion is lost, and the oversight of government and corporations is impossible.

When the shapers of this country were laying its foundation, a question of how to disallow corruption in government was an issue. After all, an entity can't employ a committee to oversee its employer— bribes, corruption, and favors would be a certainty. So, what's the answer? The citizens of America were and are once again called upon to take responsibility for the good of the country.

"The only security of all is in a free press. The force of public opinion cannot be resisted when permitted freely to be expressed," said Thomas Jefferson. "The agitation it produces must be submitted to. It is necessary, to keep the waters pure."

Jefferson was, as usual, right in his assertion that a free press is needed to "keep the waters pure." Yet when helping in the creation of this magnificent country, one thing Jefferson didn't explore was the possibility that a certain political view, seemingly bent on undermining the very principles that made America what it is—Jefferson's own principles—would monopolize the industry of the press. And, yes, you guessed it; that possibility has come true. NBC, CBS, ABC, CNN, MSNBC, and CNBC liberally monopolize the television and cable markets.

Dominated by a liberal editorial slant, these so-called news networks, whether consciously or not, advance a political and social agenda that is strikingly unfriendly to that of our Founders.

Did any of them stop to wonder why the relatively new FOX News has made such waves in the market? Maybe because they analyzed the market and found that an unbiased or even conservative-leaning network was not present. FOX filled the gap and, according to the Nielsen Ratings, has become the most-watched cable news network in America as a result. If this shows anything, it's that the news tilts so far left that right-of-center viewers are parched for coverage that doesn't sway so far left.

In the print market, you have a liberal *New York Times*, *Washington Post*, *USA Today*, *Los Angeles Times*, *Boston Globe*, *Chicago Tribune*, *Time* magazine, *Newsweek*, the dozens of subsidiaries of these media corporations, and then other liberal national, regional, and local newspapers and magazines.

On the flip side, you have a conservative *Washington Times*, *New York Post*, and a conservative *Wall Street Journal* editorial page, as well as some conservative subsidiaries of these companies. But even if you tally the other national, regional, and local papers that tend toward a conservative perspective, it's not enough to effectively compete with the other side.

Thus, while there is a "debate" in the print and television markets, it is predominantly liberal. Wouldn't you know that the dominance of modern-day liberalism in the news media has been and is seeping into the so-called reporting of the news.

The liberal bias of news reporting has become a common element of the news and is, without a doubt, present within the media. There are stacks upon stacks of evidence showing the liberal bent of the news media in America.

BIAS? I DON'T SEE ANY BIAS HERE

So who's to blame for this? The answer is simple: the reporters who are biased and the editors who are purposely injecting opinions into news stories. It sounds simple, but not simple enough for the NBC morning hosts. You see, Matt Lauer and Katie Couric don't really believe there is a bias in the news media—rather, it is the bias of the viewer!

On Phil Donahue's September 18, 2002, MSNBC program, Katie and Matt were guests. On Donahue's program, callers can call in to ask certain guests questions and be involved with the program in that way.

As the interview went along, a caller asked, "I was wondering if either Katie or Matt believes that there is a bias when delivering news media." There was confusion about the question, and the host said, "Are there . . . conservative and liberal channels and networks . . . is that your question?" Donahue complimented himself, "I'm pretty good at interpreting here."

The answer both Couric and Lauer came up with was essentially that it is only the opinions of the viewer that make people believe there is a bias. "It's all in your point of view," Matt Lauer stated. "I think that people really see what they want to . . . what they want to see from their particular frame of mind or the prism from which they're watching the program or the interview," Katie Couric followed up.

Perfect! If all else fails, blame it on someone else.

Still, more and more reporters don't even wash it down with clueless comments about prisms and perception but rather make blanket statements denying any liberal bias in the news media.

Peter Jennings, increasingly ancient anchorman for ABC, believes he is not biased at all: "I'm antibias in a very strong way."[1] And then earlier in the year, he was on *Larry King Live* and approached the subject:

"Most of the time I really think responsible journalists, of which I hope I'm counted as one, leave our bias at the side of the table."[2]

NBC News doesn't seem to think that newsman Brian Williams is biased, or at least that's what the network promo ads say: "Respected. Unbiased. In-depth. That's what makes *The News* with Brian Williams the most important news in cable."[3]

Deborah Potter, veteran in the news business and executive director of NewsLab, says, "I have yet to see a body of evidence that suggests the reporting that gets on the air reflects any political bias."[4]

Tom Brokaw joins the club, saying, "I don't think it's a liberal agenda. It happens that journalism will always be spending more time on issues that seem to be liberal to some people: the problem of the downtrodden, the problem of civil rights and human rights, the problem of those people who don't have a place at the table with the powerful."[5]

Oh, there's no bias at all—especially in Middle East news. Dan Rather only calls suicide bombers "victims."[6] Former CBS *Early Show* host Bryant Gumbel says Ariel Sharon is a man who has "done so much to oppose peace efforts in the Middle East."[7] Peter Jennings reports that a group tied to terrorist group Hamas is a "charity."[8] And NBC reporter Keith Miller went so far as to actually dub Palestinian leader Yasser Arafat as "Arafat the freedom fighter"[9] (never mind his long and documented ties to murder and terrorism).

Still, liberal bias—intended or not—is an element that has grown for years and years, so there are, as mentioned, piles of evidence with which to fill an entire book and dozens more. But for brevity's sake, here are some recent examples of liberal bias in the news media—for your reading pleasure.

JUDICIAL WATCH:
CONSERVATIVE OR NOT?

When the government watchdog group Judicial Watch has anything to do with liberals—such as, you'll remember, a suit against officials in the Clinton administration—all the major news networks make it a point to inform the viewer that the organization is conservative, thus discrediting the case by making it sound like ill-willed, partisan fighting.

Still, when the same group is involved with a lawsuit against a conservative, such as one against Vice President Dick Cheney, it morphs into an apolitical organization—at least in descriptor. Judicial Watch becomes in the journalist's estimation a "watchdog," "legal activist," and "advocacy" group. The "conservative" pejorative is dropped. Take a look at these examples:

CNN's *Inside Politics* ran a story on a federal judge ordering the missing John Huang—one of the stars in Clinton's Chinagate scandal—to be deposed by Judicial Watch. "The lawsuit concerns attempts by a *conservative* watchdog group to uncover trade documents at the Commerce Department where Huang worked until last year," reported Brooks Jackson (emphasis added).[10] In contrast, in a more recent report on litigation against Dick Cheney, Jackson said, "A Washington watchdog group is calling Vice President Richard Cheney a crook."[11]

CBS *Evening News* is involved as well. Concerning Judicial Watch litigation, Phil Jones reported, "In May, Judge Royce Lamberth issued an order to the Department of Commerce to produce documents being sought by Judicial Watch—it's a conservative group investigating foreign contributions to Democrats and the Clinton presidential campaign."[12] But in a report concerning the suit against Cheney on July 10, 2002, CBS newsman Wyatt Andrews stated, "In a gathering political storm, the President and Vice President face charges that, as businessmen, they were part of the culture that goosed up numbers to shine up companies. Vice President Cheney, already facing a six-week-old SEC investigation, was sued by a watchdog group alleging investor fraud."[13]

Running over to ABC's *World News Tonight*, in an August 27, 2001, story about Anne Marie Smith, reporter Pierre Thomas made sure the viewer realized Judicial Watch is a right-wing organization: "Today [Smith] appears to be fighting back, with support from the conservative legal foundation, Judicial Watch."[14] However, when the legal group was related to the suit against Vice President Dick Cheney, Peter Jennings forgot about it being conservative, saying, "Now to this issue of Vice

President Cheney. A legal activist group called Judicial Watch filed a lawsuit today against the Vice President and Halliburton, the energy company he used to run."[15]

NBC *Nightly News* took a spin, too, with Tom Brokaw reporting on the election mess of 2000, "Back in Florida the news media and at least one conservative advocacy group have restarted the recount."[16] Still, in another report on the same topic, Kerry Sanders said, "Florida law makes the ballots public after the election is over, and a conservative legal group, Judicial Watch, is counting here as well, trying to figure out, it says, what standard Broward officials used when they counted the ballots and found Al Gore the winner."[17] Yet when dealing with the suit against Cheney, Brian Williams told viewers, "A watchdog group that tormented the Clinton administration filed suit against Vice President Cheney over alleged accounting irregularities at Halliburton."[18]

And again, in another story on the litigation against Cheney, Campbell Brown opened, saying, "New accusations today against the Vice President and Halliburton, the massive energy company he headed for five years. The legal group, Judicial Watch, that made headlines helping Paula Jones with her lawsuit against President Clinton, today sued Vice President Cheney."[19]

The pattern is pretty obvious: when Judicial Watch is picking on Democrats, the media harp on its politics to throw into question the validity of its claims—*the case is just petty politics*, goes the line of thinking. But when Judicial Watch is going after Republicans, it's not cast as political; it's watchdoggery, legal advocacy, whatever. Anything but conservative.

APPLAUD OR BOO?
REVISIONIST HISTORY AT MTV AND VH1

This liberal bias is not only infecting itself into the news media, but also the entertainment media—a place where viewers' critical faculties are not typically on guard and young people are susceptible.

During a special July 12, 2002, edition of ABC's *20/20*, John Stossel examined the perfect example: a revised version of an October concert that was recorded for distribution by MTV and VH1. The concert, which benefited the victims of the terrorist attacks, was shown live on VH1 from Madison Square Garden. In addition, along with politicians, celebrities, and musicians, Hillary Clinton was invited to speak at the event.

When the former First Lady made her way onto the stage, a huge portion of the audience, including police and firefighters, erupted in boos and jeers. And according to an October 21, 2001, *Drudge Report*, she spent the least time on the stage (a mere twenty seconds), as she introduced a movie clip and was booed off the stage.[20]

Still, this event took an even more controversial turn as VH1 and MTV, subsidiaries of Viacom, implemented their own version of history. Stossel showed the music channel's clip of the event. There was something changed when the junior senator made her way on the stage. "Notice a difference?" asked Stossel. "The booing has been removed. Now and forever on the DVD the crowd applauds Senator Clinton."

The two hit music cable channels released a commemorative DVD that showed Hillary Clinton being overly applauded, covering the actual booing and disapproval. Not only did the media company rerun the event on VH1 showing a revised version of Clinton being applauded, but also revised it on special DVD and VHS releases!

Instead of young people being able to see and hear the genuine reaction of the audience (filled with firefighters and police officers) to her, they were left no choice but to assume that Clinton was an acceptable and well-liked figure and politician.

Unfortunately, it was a bias in the entertainment media that decided the original version of history was not appropriate and had better be prettied up for a future viewing.

REPORTERS' OPINIONS

The media bias doesn't always lie in the anchor's chair with evening newsmen injecting their obviously liberal opinions into the delivery of news. It is also in the reporter's notepad. The key part of the news media's bias is found in the political leanings of the reporters and with the opinions of editors. With evidence showing the liberal views of America's reporters, it's not a big jerk on the heart to allege liberal bias in reporting.

Still, the press is liberal and heading in the left direction. In a 1997 study, 61 percent of American newspaper reporters identified their political views as those shared by liberal Democrats; only 15 percent ID'd them as conservative.[21] Not only is the press overwhelmingly liberal, but it's becoming more liberal with every passing year. A 2001 survey and report found that a mere 6 percent of the press are conservative—down 9 percent in just four years.[22]

Although you don't have to denounce political affiliations and become apolitical when you become a news reporter, a reporter's opinion can seep into the reporting. One need only watch Tom, Peter, or Dan each night for one week to figure that out. This is not to say that liberals are the only ones who deliver biased reporting, but when less than a tenth of the news media populace is conservative, it is difficult to find a conservative reporter, much less find the bias.

POT CALLING THE KETTLE BLACK

Reporters make their biggest mistakes when they inject their opinions into the news coverage—a mistake that is not rare to find when watching news on television.

On May 8, 2002, *NBC Nightly News* ran a story by Lisa Myers that out and out bashed talk radio because it is dominated by conservatives, and in a usual "intellectual" elite belief, it is because conservatives have a small and simple view of the world.[23]

The report was about FOX News star Bill O'Reilly's plan to launch his radio career, going head-to-head with Rush Limbaugh in some markets. Lisa Myers stated, "O'Reilly joins a long list of talk radio hosts whose views range from conservative to more conservative. Why aren't there more moderate or liberal voices? Well, experts say conservatives are more entertaining because their message fits the media."

Bringing in an "expert" from *Talkers* magazine, Michael Harrison, the pundit, said, "The conservatives are more cut out for today's sound bite–oriented, short attention span, media environment."[24]

Myers wrapped up, saying, "Where others see shades of gray, O'Reilly and Limbaugh mostly portray the world as black and white—and revolving around them."

Amazing. Simply amazing.

ASHCROFT A RACIST? JENNINGS MIGHT THINK SO

In the spring of 2002, Attorney General John Ashcroft announced that the Justice Department had a plan of interviewing three thousand males that have arrived in the United States from October 1, 2001, one thousand of which the FBI and INS were unable to locate at the time.

This event should have been a usual and expected development in the post-9/11 world we live in, yet over at ABC News, it was considered ethnic profiling and maybe even racism that resulted in nothing positive.

Peter Jennings and the gang at ABC News were very unsettled on March 20, the night he reported on the story. On ABC's *World News Tonight*, opening the story, he said,

> Attorney General John Ashcroft today talked about the foreign nationals who have been questioned by law enforcement in many parts of the country since November. The Justice Department planned to interview 5,000 foreigners, most of them Arabs or Arab-Americans. Now Mr. Ashcroft says he wants another 3,000 interviews. Many of those already questioned say it was terrifying that they were, in their words, "victims of ethnic profiling."[25]

ABC News reporter Pierre Thomas reported Ashcroft's side of the story, but the reporter soon dismissed the reasoning of Ashcroft. His evidence? The opinions of two Middle Eastern males, one of which was identified as an anonymous student. "Not only did the investigations that were conducted waste police man-hours. They were ineffective and an inefficient use of law enforcement time. But they also created fear in the community," said Arab American Institute President James Zogby.[26]

In a usual "I feel your pain" opening, Thomas identified the student: "This college student who asked not to be identified says a recent meeting with police left him feeling like a criminal."

"I was just very scared, anxious, nervous, and I just wanted to get it over with," said the student. Following, Thomas reported, "He was one of several thousand men of mostly Arab descent who were interviewed . . . Justice officials say the interviews are voluntary. Critics say the interviews are voluntary in name only." Ending in the report, the anonymous student blasted the Justice Department: "My conclusion was pretty much that I don't really even have a choice because if I didn't go through with it for whatever reason, then I would be even more suspect."

Reporter Pierre concluded the story, citing a report saying that roughly twenty of those interviewed were arrested, further contributing to emotional opposition.

Now, what you're probably thinking is that this news story doesn't sound like a hard-line liberal bias news story. It has a few things here and there, and in detail, it can be defined as a liberal report, but nothing big. But what is not shown in this ABC News report is the fact that significant leads given to the FBI were found in interviewing these foreign nationals. Among them, one interviewee recalled seeing a 9/11 hijacker, and two others identified acquaintances that had taken flight training.

These facts, reported by the attorney general himself, were out and out omitted by CBS News in a news report that was in direct relation to it.

THE LIFE STORY OF DAN RATHER

If the entire adult life of Dan Rather could be summed up in one single word, that description would undoubtedly be *bias*. Rather is only the most liberally biased news reporter in the history of American journalism.

This topic runs us over to an interview between morning talk show host Don Imus and Dan Rather on his MSNBC and talk radio show, *Imus in the Morning*. This was not a typical interview and might be up in the hall of Imus fame, right next to the time Bill O'Reilly called for the murder of Matt Drudge on the show.

On Wednesday, May 22, 2002, during the political phase of "What did Bush know and when did he know it?" Dan Rather came on the show to discuss the recent events of the war on terrorism and the Bush administration. During the interview, he blasted President Bush for knowing about the events of 9/11 before they happened and defended Democrats.[27]

The CBS anchor also accused Attorney General John Ashcroft of taking advantage of insider information about terrorist warnings to fly on private jets last summer, while the public was kept in the dark about the secret alert. "If the attorney general is given information that convinces him, 'Hey, I don't want to be on any commercial airliners just now. I'm gonna take government planes everywhere,'" he said. "If the attorney general was told that . . . then it raises a question. Why wasn't the public alerted?" He also said that if the public received the Ashcroft warning, then "some people probably would not have flown."

All the events and statements he made in regard to the "Ashcroft warning" were false and possibly fabricated. You see, it took a Pentagon reporter from an entirely different network to call in to the Imus show to set the record straight.

NBC Pentagon correspondent Jim Miklaszewski called in to the show to correct Rather's story, saying that Ashcroft's decision not to fly commercial aircraft last summer was prompted by threats against his life and had no connection at all to information before September 11. But Rather wouldn't give up. He promptly scheduled another interview for Friday's show. He then blasted John Ashcroft and his aides for trying to "sully" his reputation.

When asked about Miklaszewski's correction, Rather blamed it on an effort from NBC's Tom Brokaw, Tim Russert, and Jim Miklaszewski to make him look bad. There's no bias, none at all, right, Dan?

THOSE DARN FUNDAMENTALIST CONSERVATIVE TERRORISTS!

In the spring of 2002, one of the biggest news stories running was all the anthrax letters, and with Senate offices closed, it was one of the subjects on the political front burner as well. Therefore, as predicted and expected, the news media was all over it—and why not? It was a big news story that needed to be covered. However, it was the coverage of the anthrax terrorism that got National Public Radio in trouble.

On NPR's *Morning Edition*, January 22, reporter David Kestenbaum covered the anthrax case: "Two of the anthrax letters were sent to Senators Tom Daschle and Patrick Leahy, both Democrats. One group who had a gripe with Daschle and Leahy is the Traditional Values Coalition, which, before the attacks, had issued a press release criticizing the senators for trying to remove the phrase 'so help me God' from the oath."[28]

Yes, although NPR stands for National Public Radio and, of late, being in the public arena, an organization or agency must remain unbiased. Oh! I forgot. That's only when dealing with liberals. I guess conservatives are terrorists.

This deadly mistake was picked up by, you guessed it, the Traditional Values Coalition, which sent out a press release; NPR was immediately contacted for a request for retraction and apology. Yet it took nearly a week for NPR to even officially respond. In addition, even until now, National Public Radio has yet to issue a retraction or even an apology. Instead, on January 29's *Morning Edition*, the network issued a statement saying that the report was "inappropriate."

No apology, no retraction, no action, but a lame admission that the report was "inappropriate."

CAN YOU IMAGINE A LIBERAL BENT AT THE *NY TIMES*?

When you write on liberal bias in the media, how could you forget the *New York Times*! The land of false facts, misstatements, and homosexual "marriage" announcements.

On August 8, 2002, the *Times* ran a story titled "In Twin Speeches, Bush and Cheney Vow to Fight Fraud." The report outlined the two speeches, with Cheney talking up the economy. This case was, undoubtedly, dealing with fabricated information in a story on the Bush administration tax cuts. The information presented was, laughably, used as a rebuttal to Cheney's praising the tax cuts for bringing us out of a recession.

Evelyn Neives, reporter for the *Times*, wrote,

> The vice president's speech, billed as a talk on the economy and national security, sounded at times like an address a chief executive might give to shareholders. On the economy, he said that it was now "clear from the data" that "the nation had slid into a full-blown recession" by the time he and President Bush took office, "with the economy contracting throughout the first, second and third quarters of 2001." *He credited the administration's tax cuts with helping the country to "climb out of the recession and to weather the terrible financial effects of Sept. 11," although the recession has not abated and the stock market today continued its decline* (emphasis mine).[29]

The information shown in the italicized text reports that the economy is not recovering from the recession—a counter of the words from Vice President Cheney. Yet those facts were false and fabricated.

Still, the *New York Times* finally got around to a correction. In the widely read page of corrections, they report, "An article on Aug. 8

about speeches by President Bush and Vice President Cheney defending the administration's stewardship of the economy referred incorrectly to the 2001 recession and to the direction of the stock market on Aug. 7. Economists agree that the recession has ended, not continued. The Dow Jones industrial average rose the day of the speeches, by 182 points; it did not decline."[30]

Thank God for the accuracy from the *New York Times*!

SOLUTIONS?

As you can see, the liberal monopoly of the news media is nothing short of propaganda, and if you can stand watching the big media news, it is a great cause of stress and frustration.

For some time, conservatives (or at least those who can't stand being fed lies) had no choice but to get their news from the liberal domain and yell at their television sets for thirty minutes a night or just be uninformed. However, as technological advances have been made, communication and the exchange of ideas come with the territory. The biggest success for free minds was the invention of radio.

Still, radio was dominated by the infamous liberal media conglomerates up until the late '80s when the playing field was evened up with a free market of communication. And what did the market choose? A guy who had no college degree or linkage to anything "famous," and then drove Rush Limbaugh up to syndication and a national radio program.

People were shocked to hear an average guy talk over the airwaves to millions about his opinions—his conservative opinions. This paved the way for national talk show hosts like Bob Grant, Oliver North, Dennis Prager, Sean Hannity, and dozens more.

Yet with the usefulness and the awesome power of radio, it still didn't live up to the need for a free flow of communication, news, and information. It was still run by radio show hosts that chose the content and the way it would be presented.

Enter the Internet. Anyone, from anywhere, anytime, can post opinions or information, and link to anything. It is the epitome of freedom of speech and expression. It is an amazing tool and the greatest form of communication to ever hit the planet.

The Internet is the reason a nobody named Matt Drudge came from being a cashier in a CBS gift shop to running one of the most popular news Web sites on the Net. A man without a college degree, starting with only a single Internet modem connection in an apartment in Hollywood, runs a black-and-white-text Web site at drudgereport.com.

Beginning with finding Nielsen Ratings in the trashcans of the CBS office, he posted them in Usenet message boards, found a following, and launched the Web site. Since starting the Web site with a few readers, it has now grown to millions of hits a day as Drudge gathers more and more sources. He virtually single-handedly took down the president by breaking the Monica Lewinsky story, was the first to report Bob Dole's choice of Jack Kemp for vice president on the Republican ticket, and wrote the exclusive on the merger between NBC and Microsoft to form MSNBC.

Along with instant news and the ability to know events minutes after they happen, the Internet has also been a medium of message boards or forums. In terms of politics, information, and news, FreeRepublic.com has to be the king of all sources for news, information, and the exchange of opinions and ideas. Along with being a news clipping service for politicians, talk show hosts, news reporters, and average people alike, Free Republic has been responsible for many organized protests and causes, such as the "March for Justice" rally during the Clinton impeachment hearings. This Web site and organization is quite possibly the premier and final place for what's going on in America today.

In addition, the Internet has been used for news, information, and political sites, most notably WorldNetDaily.com, NewsMax.com, TownHall.com, JewishWorldReview.com, and others.

This overview of communication through radio and Internet is vital because it must be used and continue to be used to keep the flow of information going. On the Internet, you don't need to be a multibillion-dollar corporation to own and run a Web site. However, you can make a huge difference with very little investment.

The Internet levels the playing field, because on the Net, a thirteen-year-old columnist and a forty-year-old writer can be on the same ball field as George Will and Robert Novak. However, it is the readers, the Internet users, who choose what they want, when they want it, and how they want it.

As Drudge says, you put it up and wait for people to come. The Internet is the way of the future for the news media; it will replace most all means of information. Wood pulp is being replaced by plastic, metal, and electricity.

If it weren't for the Internet, you wouldn't be reading the words that are in front of you right now. Not only did I get my start on the Internet, a lot of the information that I have researched and gathered for this book has come from it, and as I write, I have a connection to it. When a person can post anything they want millions of people to see, that is the peak of freedom. Moreover, Americans recognize that they thrive on that sort of raw information, and long for the edge that can beat the other guy.

Sure, the *Washington Post*, MSNBC, and CNN news sites are some of the most popular news sources on the Web, but why wouldn't they be, considering they constantly run ads mentioning the Web site and inform their viewers of the Web site?

Therefore, while they have a substantial amount of visitors, it is going down, and alternate sources are being chosen, as Drudge is growing up to five million hits a day, WorldNetDaily grows in size and readership—now a top-1,000 Web site according to Web-tracking site Alexa.com—and dozens of other sites also do extremely well.

No cynicism intended, but the old media is gone. It's too late to reform the system and bring back a balanced view. Unless someone has $100 million around and no use for it, it is literally impossible for an independent media outlet to be created.

Except for FOX News, of course, the old media is of no value. Although the Internet is still a baby, all the major stories are broke on-line now. And because the Internet is still in a forming stage, it must be invaded, taken over, and used for good by conservatives.

Would this make the Internet totally biased with nothing but a conservative spin? No. Because real, pure conservatism is truth and the fight to find the truth of politics and news. In order to fight liberal monopolized media conglomerates, every possible forum and medium must be used in this struggle.

FURTHER READING

Books

- Kristina Borjesson, *Into the Buzzsaw: Leading Journalists Expose the Myth of a Free Press* (Amherst: Prometheus, 2002).
- Ann H. Coulter, *Slander: Liberal Lies About the American Right* (New York: Crown, 2002).
- Matt Drudge, *Drudge Manifesto* (New York: New American Library, 2002).
- Bernard Goldberg, *Bias: A CBS Insider Exposes How the Media Distort the News* (Washington, DC: Regnery, 2001).

Web Sites

- www.mrc.org
- www.drudgereport.com
- www.accuracyinmedia.org
- www.worldnetdaily.com
- www.newsmax.com
- www.townhall.com
- www.jewishworldreview.com

Sound Off

★ EDUCATION ★

4

A Liberal Education

EDUCATION IS ONE OF THE BIGGEST ISSUES IN OUR NATION. From the local school board meetings and decisions to the national debates in Congress, it's an issue we all know. Yet, as with almost all issues, it is important mainly because it has problems. The educational system of America is beset with many troubles and failings that, when coupled with its high expectations, propel it to the center stage of the national debate.

The trend goes back for years, socially and academically. Both moral erosion and suffering SAT scores began in the middle 1960s. With the latter, things were so bad by the 1970s that during Jimmy Carter's administration, the debate went from random political talk to a full-blown national issue that became crucial to getting elected. As a favor to our great friends at the National Education Association, Carter created the Department of Education.

Not that it helped in the long run. Today, scores still suffer, and the massive, cumbersome bureaucracy can barely continue to exist, much less educate millions of restless kids around the country. It's an impossibility to run such an intricate, vital, and crucial agency at the national level. Tell me, please, if there is any logic in allowing legislators from Capitol Hill with little to no experience in education to attempt to control the education in every single government school in the United States of America.

The idea does not work for *real* education, but it sucks up money from everybody: businesses, the American people, the federal budget, and state budgets. Yet some organizations have positioned themselves to use that power to force their warped agendas into American life and culture. Legislation is used as a hand by the NEA, and representatives in Washington become puppets when it comes to education. Money talks, that's for sure, and money wins and loses elections.

Looking at the NEA's massive budgets, you know what I'm getting at. The resolutions passed at the NEA's little annual party end up becoming law. There's something wrong and fundamentally undemocratic about that; apparently, liberals complain about every special interest except their own. It's not only a rip-off; it's also immoral and unethical. And it should be illegal since the Constitution leaves education up to the states.

Jimmy Carter sure did the NEA a favor.

Since then, education has grown at an enormous rate. In public schools, about $6,000 to $10,000 is spent per pupil, per year. Ironically, a homeschooled family can spend less than $1,000 a year for homeschooling the family and, as we'll see in the next chapter, usually with better results.

The system is bloated. It doesn't work. It sucks up resources. It's illegitimate. And it's unconstitutional. In the present state, it's also immoral, unethical, and nothing less than an attack on American institutions and values. Federal control of education is nearly impossible to manage, regardless of good intentions.

THE SYSTEM

This is what happens: around 7:45 A.M., millions of children from around the nation pack up their backpacks, grab lunch (if their lunch is even made at home), and get on the bus or drive off to their local government education institution.

So, school starts around 8:30. They go from class to class, like robots in a factory, until around 12:00 P.M. Then, thanks to the very generous legislators on Capitol Hill for spending our money, they eat government food that is mandated by the school lunch program. Afterward, they go back to the routine from class to class, sometimes taking in knowledge (other times not), and then 3:00 P.M. *finally* rolls around. Do they go home? Maybe, but not too often.

If you don't have anyplace to go after school, you can stay into the evening for those wonderful after-school programs. Many kids stay for sports games or practice after school.

Then, maybe around 6:00 P.M. they end up heading home—if they're lucky. Yet many students will end up heading over to a friend's house or doing something else. In any case, American government students leave early in the morning, head home late, spend hours on homework, and go to bed. They repeat this process five days a week.

It starts early. Students are thrown together with hundreds of schoolmates at the tender age of five. Their lives are run by mandated tests, mandated curricula, mandated educational topics, mandated class times, and even the mandated food they must eat! It's like a processing factory. You have so many classes that take up so much time and homework that must be done at a certain time as well as required reading and work.

This rigid schedule is not interesting, not fun, not an educational environment, not healthy, and not the love that a child needs. With this, the students end up growing apart from their parents; in this environment arguments and fights not only happen, but are actually encouraged by what the culture says teenagers are *supposed* to be like.

In addition, by throwing these hundreds of children together, a type of society is created. With societal morals as tattered as ours have become, this spells trouble from the start. In an effort to be on the top of the pack or become notable, a student must compromise values (if he even has any to begin with). This means profanity, sex, immorality, unethical actions, and sometimes illegal actions. Presto! The so-called innocence of children is wiped out.

Yes, there's more. As far as academics go, if other students can't keep up with the pace at which everyone else is "learning," the entire class slows up, resulting in boredom, restlessness, and an overall negative environment. Children excel when they are challenged. It can be difficult for the teacher when half the class can't keep up. The usual response is to cater to the lowest common denominators.

Children are dealt with the same way animals are! It's not only despicable but a disgusting sight. The students are then thrown into a society of high standards—college. Many are not ready for those high standards and are forced to take remedial courses or risk failure. In many cases, colleges are now starting to lower their standards to meet the needs of uneducated public school students.

THE RESULTS

After the children are processed through this system of education, what happens next? By mandate, they take tests to see who's smart and who's . . . well . . . not so smart.

In California, for example, they aren't doing too well in that field. More than half the students who took the state's required test for receiving a diploma failed the test! In March of 2001, California students also scored only 52 percent on the state's standardized test.[1]

The test scores apparently are getting so bad in New York that in 2002, school superintendents around the state sent letters with students to the college admissions offices telling them to ignore test scores.[2] The average score on standardized tests around the United States is about 50 percent, while the ACT scores are near the basement, in the area of the lower 20s. In North Carolina, a mere 48 percent of fourth graders could pass a simple and single essay test.[3]

Although these results are devastating, it's no fault of children. What is funny (not ha-ha funny but hmm funny), however, is that we teach teens these things, they fail, and then they are blamed for being less than smart and are shunned.

THE PROBLEMS

There are many problems in the public education system. However, as we just discovered, it all comes down to the fact that the schools' results just plain stink.

Who's to blame? Teachers? The system? A piece of legislation? I'd have to choose all of the above—almost. Teachers definitely aren't to blame for the overall problems of education. Every time I mention my opinion on issues facing the United States education system, I get letters from people with views all over the spectrum—from praises and agreements, to e-mails attempting to convince me that the system is acceptable and almost perfect. I have received many e-mails from teachers who believe I am attacking them. Additionally, I receive letters from public school advocates who shun me for attacking teachers.

The fact is, the charge is unfounded. Never have I, nor will I generally attack the public school teachers of America. Instead, I wish to greatly reform the current system. In the business world, if there are problems in your business, you initially analyze the problems, find solutions, and reform the system. The notion of firing large groups of employees to fix a problem is absurd. However, if problems continue, you secondly want to analyze the actions of employees.

We all must realize that most teachers are not out with an agenda—except to teach kids. Public school teachers are some of the most underpaid workers in America; therefore, teachers are obviously not out to get rich. I don't know why we call elected officials "public servants," but if any group does deserve the name, it is the teachers.

We see public school advocates and members of the Left hide behind these public servants when the system is attacked.

You cannot convince me that there aren't thousands upon thousands of frustrated and unsatisfied schoolteachers out there. The system requires them to do a tough job but prohibits them from administering real work and discipline to their students. Likewise, many parents today force teachers to raise their children from first grade all the way up through senior year in high school. However, when teachers push and challenge their students to do work, the parents attack the teachers! The same people who put them in that place are not allowing them to do their job efficiently.

One school counselor wrote me with this dilemma: "Administrators are frustrated and unfortunately lack support. They can discipline the student for refusing to work, but that leads to suspensions. The child is safer at school than at home without supervision." My solution to her problem was to administer tougher and greater discipline. Unfortunately, that is discouraged, if not outright prohibited.

Does anyone call this a real "punishment"? Why are teachers forced into the position of raising children but not allowed to enforce essential disciplinary action? Because the U.S. education system is in disarray. If the teachers are to raise America, they should be allowed to use greater discipline. Remember, discipline is just another type of instruction, one aimed at leading children to later maturity. Teaching without using discipline is an oxymoron. Learning is not just math, science, history, etc., but it is also work ethic, patience, and organization skills. Giving teachers more latitude here is just common sense.

While not all teachers are suitable for teaching, more often than not, the schoolteachers are ready and willing. If we can reform the system to allow teachers *real* control over the classroom, more will go into the field of teaching. The thought of attempting to control a fifth-grade classroom while being prohibited from using discipline and punishment does not sound very attractive.

No, I am not attacking public school teachers. It is the system that I am attacking. Teachers, parents, and students are all frustrated—with good reason. There *is* a problem. We must decentralize the education monster, increase local control, and demand more parent or guardian involvement. By doing so we will greatly reduce special-interest control (like the NEA's) that adds to the chaos while also getting programs and support more closely tailored to the needs of individual schools and students.

I invite schoolteachers and administrators to let me know about their feelings on what's going on here. If large numbers of people are out to "help" the children, you can really help by not standing for the injustice children are being served. Their chances of becoming successful are reduced every day. We must put an end to this.

Abraham Lincoln once noted that "the philosophy of the school room in one generation will be the philosophy of government in the next." Do you really want our future generations to lack in common sense, discipline, organization skills, values, and work ethic?

The real problem is that our standards are not high enough. We must raise the bar; we must demand more from students. All the while doing this, we also must help students reach that bar of success with love and support.

CHILDREN: THE ULTIMATE POLITICAL PAWN

If you're part of a program or initiative, or you cosponsor a bill that looks as if it is working hard to help children, you'll be looked upon as a good person because it comes across as a "good thing" when adults help those "who can't help themselves." Indeed, those who help those in need are laudable. But in the ever-hectic political world, there only must *appear* to be some caring thought behind an initiative for it to look acceptable. Appearance becomes everything.

Congress, every year, complicates the system. The truth is, most of the things done do not help at all. The only ones gaining something here are the politicians who support these "caring" initiatives. They get reelected, their buddies pat them on the back, and they get another paycheck.

Keep in mind, they always say it's "for the young people." *Of course, it is.* How could anyone vote against the children?

In our society, people tell kids that they're not smart enough and that they will understand when they're older. So, the world tells me to be silent, that I should be seen rather than heard. In the Campaign

Finance Reform legislation that was passed in 2002, for example, there was a provision that would prohibit anyone seventeen or younger from donating a dime to a political campaign. Congress to children: *be quiet.*

I'll be the first to testify that the majority of people out to help children are not helping at all. In fact, they're messing up the whole system. The people who lose in all this are the children.

It would be irresponsible and a lie to make a blanket statement about those involved by saying that they are all out for personal gain. However, many are. Naturally, not all people are out to rip off my generation. It's people like my parents who have taught me themselves, citizens who work hard when participating in the local school system, and those like them who work for *real* education. But it is sad to say that most people do not have a genuine and pure care for young people. The fact is, the young generation and the kids still in school are being used. Instead of reforming or abolishing the inept education system, many are out to further their personal or political lives.

Relatively speaking, I realize the current federal education system hasn't been in place very long, but it definitely has been in place long enough to create an effective system. It hasn't done so. In addition, with the billions of dollars that flow through the education system, it should at least be acceptable. It's not. In Washington, D.C., money is pouring into that school system to the tune of approximately $10,000 per pupil, per year. But even with that, it is not an effective system—far from it.

Instead of reducing federal control and expanding local management abilities, Congress has created a monster. With a federally centralized system and department, the Department of Education is in total chaos.

If results are anything to go by, the education bureaucrats in Washington seem to care more about creating a dumbed-down society in order to create a more submissive nation rather than creating a healthy learning atmosphere and producing independent thinkers.

The way politicians are using young people to advance their political careers has largely gone unnoticed. So we, the people, must realize that the goal of our government officials is not to create an education system that works. While the young people—the future of this nation—are being ripped off, our "representatives" on the Hill are furthering their political agendas. It is further evidence that education is not an issue that many politicians sincerely care about but use to stay elected and gain power.

CULTURE INFLUENCE

We have all these problems associated with American education, from pathetic test scores to the problems associated with the school-age society, but just when you thought it couldn't get any worse . . .

As referenced in the first chapter, a special congressional committee in 1954 reported that in something like fifteen years, a society could be completely changed, "the time it takes to inculcate a new culture into a rising crop of youngsters." Prophetic words from Congress that year, as special-interest groups around the nation took notice. Without a doubt, these days, the National Education Association is the authority on shaping the culture of America.

The NEA has such a strong grip of control on the educational process in America, it's truly amazing. Yet that feeling stops when you take a look at the record.

It has continually, throughout the years, taken advantage of that to force its agenda of humanism, liberalism, and anti-Americanism. By so doing the NEA has successfully changed our culture for the worse.

Another thing to add to culture influence is revisionist history. Kids are taught the lie of Abraham Lincoln growing up in a log cabin and being "Honest Abe," Franklin Delano Roosevelt is hailed as one of the greatest heroes in our history, and no one ever speaks of the amazing unconstitutional legislation and ideas our legislators and presidents have pushed.

This is very much like the issue of the separation of church and state. The education system shouldn't be interfering in the American culture as it is, but culture should be able to shape education. Otherwise, it's nothing but brainwashing and indoctrination from an agenda to change our culture in some way. It's obvious what's happening here. From homosexuality, to liberalism, to abortion, America's youth are being influenced on these passionate issues and are failing to meet the grade on learning.

HOMOSEXUALITY

Homosexuality and the homosexual community have a great stranglehold on America's culture. Through the entertainment industry and political special-interest groups, homosexuality has been acceptable to many in leadership roles across the country.

However, the view on homosexuality is beginning to change. Although the revolution of the '60s and '70s spawned a new society that tolerates and encourages tolerance for almost everything, society and culture seem to be taking a more realistic approach to life—even if it only seems like a nudge in that direction now.

Groups such as the National Education Association, National Organization for Women, and Planned Parenthood know this. Moreover, they are acting on it by promoting their views in the public schools of America.

In the 2000–2001 NEA Adopted Resolutions, the group promoted "multiculture" education in an effort to reduce "racism," "homophobia," and all other forms of discrimination. Likewise, the homosexual community, having anecdotal evidence to support its claim of widespread homophobia, pushes for legislation that mandates the teaching of homosexuality in government schools.

Yet it goes much farther than that. Homosexuality is not only *taught* in public schools; it is portrayed as an acceptable lifestyle and act—and those who believe it is a sin are homophobic hate-mongers.

Although there is no hard evidence suggesting that homosexuals are constantly being attacked verbally and physically, the NEA has attempted to present evidence saying so. But even though its research is full of holes, for the sake of argument, let us concede the point that there *is* widespread discrimination against homosexuals in public schools.

Taking it a step farther, let us also imagine there is a widespread prejudice toward Christianity and Christians. In order to combat that, public school system officials wouldn't even think of teaching the history of Christianity and explaining that Christianity is a great and acceptable lifestyle and religion. Yet they do this with homosexuality.

Even without political pressure, school administrators and teachers would probably treat each "homophobic" discrimination case independently and use disciplinary action, if necessary. That's exactly what happened when anti-Semitism and discrimination against blacks were widespread. Given that, we can see that in order to put a stop to "homophobia," we don't have to teach that homosexuality is an acceptable or good thing. Schools just have to deal with each case as it arises, individually.

If the word *religion* were behind the homosexual lifestyle, there would be a huge public outcry, forcing the prohibition of homosexuality in public schools. However, there is no public outcry because homosexuality is not a religion, although it is objectionable to many parents of faith around the country.

America is filled with a war of words. Doublespeak, disinformation, and propaganda are an epidemic in the political and cultural world of America. The unfortunate aspect of this particular case is that unaware and innocent children are losing from it. The so-called hate crime prevention programs in schools are an excuse for promoting homosexuality and just another way to force the homosexual agenda into the open. Under the name of "tolerance," "school safety," and "multiculturalism," children are being indoctrinated to believe that the homosexual lifestyle is legitimate and acceptable.

Reported in Focus on the Family's *Citizen:*

Marin County, just north of San Francisco via the Golden Gate Bridge, is one of the most affluent counties in the nation, with a median home price of $529,000. Home to U.S. Sen. Barbara Boxer, it's also one of the most liberal. When Californians voted overwhelmingly for Proposition 22, placing the state on record against same-sex "marriages," Marin was one of only four counties to buck the tide.

Even so, Marin has its relatively conservative enclaves. Drive to the northernmost city of Novato (population 47,000), with its lower home prices and family-friendly atmosphere, and you'd think you were in a typical modest-sized American town. So when Greg and Lisa sat down to dinner one evening in late February and asked their fourth-grade son, Kenny, to tell them about his school day, they weren't ready for what they heard.

"We had an assembly today," Kenny said. "We learned that there are all kinds of families," including "two mommies" and "two daddies." He also shared some of the words he'd learned for the first time that day: *homosexual, lesbian, faggot.*

Kenny wasn't the only child to bring home such a report. All the second- through fifth-graders at Pleasant Valley School had been called to an assembly, where they learned slogans like "I'm gay and it's OK," reinforced by various skits—like one in which Rapunzel cut her hair and ran away with her girlfriend. The show made an impact. "Daddy, am I a lesbian?" one third-grade girl asked. "I like girls better than boys." The group behind the assembly bore an innocent-sounding name, Cootie Shots. But it turned out to be an offshoot of Fringe Benefits, a theater group that gets public funds for "tolerance of diversity" performances in high schools and middle schools throughout the Los Angeles Unified School District. Now the group is targeting much younger kids, because—in the words of a longtime Fringe Benefits booster, Steven Hicks of the Gay, Lesbian and Straight Education Network (GLSEN) of Los Angeles—"It is imperative to begin addressing these issues in the elementary schools as early as possible."[5]

Enough said.

SEX EDUCATION

For over thirty years, the nation has debated on the assumption that giving sex education to our teenagers would reduce the number of abortions and teen pregnancy. I'm not so sure the debate is needed. The assumption is equivalent to handing an irresponsible child a gallon of gasoline and a box of matches. Anyone who has been a teenager should know that.

Around the country, schools give teens the information of sex—sex education. They hand out free condoms. They additionally allow access to birth control and even abortions. Unless the teens are taught that sex outside marriage is wrong and believe in sexual abstinence until they tie the knot, then what on earth do you think is going to happen?

Assuming abortions and teen pregnancy will decline with more sex education assumes first that teens are responsible, moral, and have family values. Bad idea—especially when applied to boys. Trust me. You can't assume or rely on common sense from a massive group of teens; it will always come back to bite you.

Unfortunately, these practices continue around the country, with "health" conferences and presentations in science classes. The way things are going, the basic message to children is this: go have sex.

Sex educators don't sufficiently speak of the consequences of actions or what may happen if things go wrong. If things do, you have two options: murder or raise a child through high school and college. Why can't schools simply be moral or responsible? The simple answer is that abstinence education may be *religious*. Oh, the horror! Government schools can avoid the whole entanglement by letting the right people deal with the subject matter from the get-go.

Sex education is something that should be left between a child and his or her parents. There are enough public awareness campaigns to take care of the rest.

FIXING THE PROBLEM

After reading this, it is undeniable that our national educational system is in complete shambles. So what are we to do? The test scores don't add up, the system is sucking up billions of dollars, and we continue to do nothing. No, more mandated tests won't fix it. Neither will more legislation. Even new regulations won't!

Radical change is required to fix the dying education system. Otherwise, the only options are private schools and homeschooling. I examine those two alternatives to traditional public education in the next chapter. But for the moment let's look at what not to do: lower standards.

Instead of analyzing why students have low test scores, looking at the problem, and finding a solution, all too often we simply lower the standards ("There, now you can get that B+ without studying! Don't you feel better about yourself?"). Further, teachers are afraid to put pressure on their pupils in order for them to learn because many are being threatened by parents. In the end, schools get dumbed down, and as we saw earlier in the chapter, kids have to carry letters telling prospective colleges to ignore their dismal test scores.

When you upgrade rules to make them tougher and improve the standards, the results are obviously going to be superior. Looking at the standards of the schools in the eighteenth and nineteenth centuries, you can see why generation after generation was very intelligent and mature. If you look at our Founding Fathers, for example, they were some of the brightest people that ever lived. They were very intelligent and capable because they were held to very tough standards. Most of them were homeschooled and had very tough lives. Out of their lives, many of them developed integrity, intelligence, honesty, and courage. As a result of the standards and rules they were held accountable to, America was created.

We must focus on the results and work harder to help people meet them rather than lower the standards to meet those who don't.

But even that is in a sense superficial. Beyond keeping high standards, we need to realize that education is no business of the federal government. You may be thinking that I'm wrong on this issue, but the people who created the federal government believed it was a state issue as well; Article 1, Section 8, which spells out the duties of Congress, says nothing about education. With good reason.

A federal department of anything can be run and maintained by special-interest groups with ulterior motives. Don't tell me that all the interest from the NEA, NOW, Planned Parenthood, and the load of other organizations doesn't get play. Remember Congress's conclusion that, in fifteen years, an entire culture could be made over by inculcating ideas into the minds of young people through education? Well, this is exactly what's going on in our schools. Education in America is working exactly as it's supposed to, from the direction of special interest.

The Department of Education has become nothing but an Orwellian Department of Culture.

We look at all the problems and continue to debate. However, the group with the most control of the debate, the National Education Association, doesn't want it changed. Its goal in education is to shape views and opinions to align with its own—by and large, a socialistic, humanistic vision of America—and it uses the Ed Department to bring its vision about.

Thus, the first substantive thing that must be done is probably an impossible goal. The federal Department of Education must be destroyed. This will not only cut down on the monster and the bureaucracy it brings, but will also shake the *grasp* of special-interest control on schools.

The second thing to do is forbid any education legislation from Congress. It's not the job of Congress to do these things. Not only is it unconstitutional, but I fail to see the logic or success in controlling schools that are thousands of miles away.

Third, we must revamp the state education departments. Completely restructure, reevaluate, and reappropriate. The state departments of education also rely heavily on the federal Department of Education, so reorganization would be needed. Furthermore, many state departments are also huge monsters that must be tamed.

Fourth, the deregulation of the educational system is needed. I know many teachers whose lives are nearly a complete headache because of all the regulations they must follow that completely inhibit certain aspects of teaching.

Additionally, we need to use vouchers. By applying a private sector rule and merging the public schools into the same field as the private schools, it will bring about competition. Competition is always a good thing if you're looking for a better product.

Last, parental involvement is a requirement. I realize that you can't legislate such a thing, but it spawns from responsibility. Maybe if we can turn our educational system around and start to teach real knowledge—reading, writing, arithmetic, and history, as well as the Constitution and the values our nation was founded on—we can instill responsibility.

Real and sincere local control is the solution—period. Communities can take care of themselves without Big Daddy telling them what to do. Local control can fix local problems and issues. Politicians in Washington sure aren't going to.

When we hit the bottom line, the real solution is just to be honest. Truth will fix problems, and it will radically shape systems. Cut the deceit and the lies; come down to what the education system really is and how to fix it. Enough debate.

Do it for the children—for real this time.

FURTHER READING

Books

- William J. Bennett, Chester E. Finn Jr., and John T. E. Cribb Jr., *The Educated Child: A Parent's Guide, from Preschool Through Eighth Grade* (New York: Free Press, 1999).

- John Taylor Gatto, *A Different Kind of Teacher: Solving the Crisis of American Schooling* (Berkeley, CA: Berkeley Hills Books, 2002).

- Peter Kline, *Why America's Children Can't Think* (Makawao, Maui, HI: Inner Ocean Publishing, 2002).

- Christina Hoff Sommers, *The War Against Boys: How Misguided Feminism Is Harming Our Young Men* (New York: Simon & Schuster, 2000).

- Thomas Sowell, *Inside American Education: The Decline, the Deception, the Dogmas* (New York: Free Press, 1993).

5

Alternative Learning

AFTER SEEING THE STATE OF THE PUBLIC EDUCATION system, the logical response is a question of alternatives. Are we stuck in this godforsaken system of public education? Absolutely not. Alternative education—that is, an alternative to government schools—has much under its name. The following are three examinations of alternatives to the failing government school system.

PRIVATE SCHOOLS

Private schools have been known for higher standards of educational excellence, moral and religious teaching, smaller classes, greater parent involvement, safer environment, and teachers that are more qualified. This all leads to one thing: *a better option than government schools*. Unfortunately, because parents who wish to send their children to private schools must pay tuition on top of the school taxes they already pay, many parents are priced out of the market.

The main reason voucher advocates say their idea works—allowing parents to take a portion of their money paid in taxes as tuition to a school (a voucher)—is because a voucher program creates competition between a variety of different schools. The competition requires staff, administration, and teachers to work harder in an effort to create a better option for students. Private education illustrates that life in America is all about money—and it talks.

Private schools are a better option than government schools because they do not receive an endless flow of money regardless of performance, as their counterparts in the public education arena do. Therefore, they have to make the tuition a parent is paying worth the money by producing better educational experiences and results.

Private academies and schools are very much like colleges. The enrollment in more prestigious schools, many times, costs a good deal, and the school is looking for students that will gain something from the school and later in life accomplish a great deal, which allows the school or academy to brag.

Noninclusive

Several features are unique to private schools and set them apart as good alternatives to government schooling. For starters, private schools are noninclusive. Along with requiring a standard of excellence among the student body, they also require certain standards with the parents of the students, especially with private religious schools.

One example that caused a great stir across the national news was the so-called stripper mom. The mother of a five-year-old girl became a stripper while her daughter was enrolled in a private, religious school—something that was strictly prohibited by the enrollment contract that parents sign. Although controversy surrounded the whole case, Capital Christian School in Sacramento, California, allowed the daughter to remain in attendance but required the mom to quit stripping—which she did.[1]

In addition to strict enrollment guidelines, private schools have the right to use discipline. Many times, areas pertaining to discipline are included in a contract and allow the school to use discipline at its discretion. Because these guidelines are inserted into the contract, the teacher does not have to worry about a hulking lawsuit breathing fire down on him. Furthermore, with this ability to use discipline—

much unlike public schools—it allows the teacher to better direct the education of his students by training children to focus and learn, or at least not distract others from doing so.

And private school teachers tend to be less aloof than government school teachers simply because there are fewer students in relation to the number of teachers. With most private schools, there is a student population cap. Therefore, the ratio of students to a teacher is substantially smaller than their counterpart, the public school system.

Money is one of the reasons for this. While most who go to private schools are not filthy rich, living in a three-story mansion with a butler, the tuition costs are still not cheap. Looking at the financial sacrifices a family has to willingly make hints at the greater motivation they have to get involved in the educating of their children. Couple that motivation with the great incentive of making sure their hard-earned money doesn't go to waste, and parents of private schoolers tend to be more involved in their children's educational experience than in a "free" public school.

Public and private schools do share many similarities. The class setups are similar. And, unfortunately, so are the educational results in some cases. Initially, you would believe that the results of private education would be substantially higher, yet that is not the case. The results are not substantially better than public education. However, while the results are somewhat better in relation to their peers in government schools, the strict discipline will stay with them.

Not that the differences are entirely negligible; the market sees to that. The ultimate reason private schools function more efficiently than public schools is that if they don't, they're out of business. It's the simple concept of the free market. With their competition having a great deal of endless funding (in fact, the worse government schools perform, the more money allotted to help improve them; talk about perverse incentives—getting paid for poor performance), it requires an even greater job performance.

Standards

The standards at many private schools are extremely high. Besides having to pay substantial amounts of money for tuition, enrollment in private schools usually requires referrals, history, and transcripts of previous school years. The livelihood of the school and the employment of the staff at the school depend on having responsible and eager learners enroll at the private school.

Let's say you own a hardware store, for example, which you started with your own money and worked hard to make successful. While it's unconstitutional for the government to support a private business, for the sake of argument, let's say that down the street there's a government-supported hardware store competing with you by offering very cheap supplies. In order to keep your store in business, you and your employees have to work much harder in order to provide service and supplies of such high quality you can profit while still charging more than your competitor.

This is what goes on with private schools. The private school has to work much harder at getting quality teachers, higher standards on enrollment, quality students, and a better educational experience than the "free" public school down the street.

This all leads to better standards in the choice of teachers, requires the enrollment of particularly eager learners with good track records, and leads to a less bureaucratic administration—the overhead for which is too costly and the processes of which are too inefficient for a private business going head-to-head with a state-subsidized competitor.

But beyond high academic standards and performance, one of the great reasons for choosing private education is the religious aspect of the school or academy. As religion is an irreplaceable aspect of American life and culture, it is very important to most families that it be coupled along with their children's education. Indeed, a strong world-and-life view is foundational to any lasting education.

Conclusion

Private education has been shown to produce better-quality students than the competition in the public sector. There are many reasons, but the main two are that (1) private schools are noninclusive and can enforce their high standards with discipline and strictness not typically allowed in public schools; and (2) because of the competitive nature of the market, private schools have to perform well or they cease operating. The end result is that private schools tend to produce well-disciplined graduates and actually teach their students. Amazing, isn't it?

CHARTER SCHOOLS

Since the 1980s when Ronald Reagan inspired the devolution of federal power back to the American people, a push to decentralize and disassemble central forms of government has been a strong force. The decentralization and push for power to be brought back to local government have not only been seen in government management, but also in the educational system.

In the 1990s, we saw a radical desire to deconstruct the institutions of education and create a decentralized system of local control and parental involvement. However, that reform initiative would be nearly impossible to bring about inside the traditional public education system. As a result, the idea of charter schools became a plan and a reality. This educational movement includes both conservatives who believe in individual competition in the free market and liberals growing impatient with the ineffective public schools.

Background

Charter schools are, as homeschooling, a topic of which our country is largely ignorant. But that is to be expected when there are only about 2,700 charter schools in the country with approximately 275,000 students.[2]

Although the essence of charter schools is very much private, they involve public education and government regulations. Charter schools are mostly supported by public funds but are only minimally accountable to public authority—public schools with private-school benefits.

The schools are sponsored by a local or state educational organization that observes their results and management of the schools. Unlike their traditional public school counterparts, however, these schools are allowed to operate freely from the bureaucratic messes that destroy education and are not served with an endless list of regulations.

Each of these autonomous schools has its own charter that structures its operations instead of the state education codes. To start a school, the founder(s) must petition to receive a charter from the local school board or from the state education department.

Once up and running, charter schools operate much like private schools. The school is noninclusive and has discretion over the children it accepts. In some cases, a lottery is used if there are more applicants than classroom seats available. The schools are run by teachers, parents, educational entrepreneurs, and community leaders whose hands are not tied by the myriad statutory rules, program regulations, and union contracts that often hamper the school boards and principals that truly want school reform.

Because they are mostly private, the way education is carried out is left up to the discretion of the teacher, and so there is usually not a mainstream curriculum or education method. Moreover, because charter schools rarely are inclusive, the class size is smaller, and the teacher has greater power over the classroom and more interaction with students.

Additionally, with private groups monitoring their success, or lack thereof, the schools are judged on the results that are produced. If the school is not educating and operating adequately, the school is closed. There is usually a review by the charter agency every three to five years. Usually, the charter statutes require this review before the school can be rechartered. Sometimes state law requires that students participate in statewide testing, follow curricular guidelines, and the schools must submit financial statements annually.

Results

Charter schools, as a whole, are doing fairly well. Sixty-five percent of the schools have an average waiting list of about 130 students.[3]

Still, the actual test results that charter schools produce are in question and may be even lower than public schools, some reports claim. According to one news report,

> Students in charter schools, often seen as an alternative to failing neighborhood schools, are scoring significantly below public school pupils in basic reading and math skills, a new study shows.
>
> Charter school students were anywhere from a half year to a full year behind their public school peers, researchers at the Brookings Institution concluded after reviewing 1999–2000 reading and math achievement test scores of 376 charter schools in 10 states.[4]

Yet this claim may not be all that it seems. You see, many charter schools specialize in helping underachieving students to achieve academic success. Amazingly, about half of those who performed "poorly" (as judged by their parents) are now "excellent" or "above average" in the charter school.[5]

Therefore, it is hard to put a firm pinpoint on the success of charter schools. With so many poorly performing students joining these schools, to draw the conclusion that charter schools are themselves failing on a wide scale based upon this report is not credible—the Brookings Institution even conceded that charter schools may be performing better than the report shows.

As with homeschooling, the scientific results and success of charter schools cannot be proved. As with homeschoolers, not all those who get their education at home or in these schools go to college or take college tests. Additionally, the test results of these students are often kept private.

However, the tangible factors in finding the success of charters are the reactions from those involved. Fifty-seven percent of parents with children enrolled in charter schools believe that their school year has been above average to excellent.[6]

Furthermore, most students and parents are of the opinion that their participation in these schools has been positive. According to the Hudson Institute's Charter Schools in Action Project, 60 percent of about 5,000 students report that their charter school teachers are better than their former teachers. In addition, over 60 percent of parents say that their charter school is better than their child's previous school with respect to class size, school size, and individual attention from teachers.

Conclusion

With charter schools still being much of a new phenomenon, I think it is safe to say that we are not fully educated about them. With their growth in the years to come, we will be learning more and more about them as their progress and results are unveiled. But up front, this type of education is ideally the model for reform in traditional public schools, with radical decentralization, privatization, local control, and extreme deregulation.

HOMESCHOOLING

Since the beginning of the so-called homeschooling revolution, the total population of the homeschooling community has grown to just a shave under a million people—and this is considered one of the lowest reported numbers.[7] Despite the small numbers, though, homeschoolers have made waves among mainstream America, with great controversy over socialization and the results of a homeschooler in day-to-day business later in life.

The worries are unfounded. Many homeschooled children and teens have gone off to well-known institutes of higher learning and finally taken leadership positions in local, state, and federal government.

But where those who have been educated at home stir up the most controversy and directly threaten the "traditional" educating of the twentieth and twenty-first centuries is in the field of academic results. Here homeschoolers have obviously threatened the liberals' nest at the National Education Association. The negative reaction by the NEA was shown when it decided that "home schooling programs cannot provide the student with a comprehensive education experience."[8]

Yet no matter the negatives from the opponents of homeschooling (the criticism, the downplaying, and even the direct assault on a parent's right to homeschool), children educated at home have continued to beat the expectations, and many Americans are turning back to the historic roots of their country.

History

As a certain writer suggested to me, some believe that the "phenomenon" known as "homeschooling" is a new idea to suddenly hit this nation and create a revolution of parents and teachers. But homeschooling is nowhere near a new phenomenon. The Founding Fathers of our country were not only some of the most intelligent and brightest men to ever live, but many of those past presidents were homeschooled.

Don't tell the NEA this (or, actually, yes, please do), but the Constitution never allowed for a Department of Education. Why? The Constitution never provided for a federal Department of Education because the Founders knew of the great threat that it could be to the liberties and freedoms of this country. If a set of like-minded organizations could influence legislators and force their agenda through education, the results would be devastating, as we are seeing in America today.

Therefore, the logical choice was to educate children at home—which was done during colonial times and up through the eighteenth century. Obviously, the socialization aspect of their home education didn't inhibit them from creating the greatest country to ever hit the face of the earth, and—dare I suggest?—it may have actually helped them along the way.

Respect

I don't mean to boast about homeschoolers and their results. Well, actually, I do, because homeschoolers have done nothing but earn the little respect that has been granted them. The homeschooling community has never been given the respect it fully deserves, though other education methods have, despite the fact that their results leave much to be desired. All this is to say that homeschoolers definitely have not had it handed to them on a silver platter. They've had to fight all the way.

In recent history, when the homeschooling revolution began, the dignity and respect of homeschoolers and their parents were continually hammered by many in mainstream education. Whether politically or legally, the rights of homeschoolers have also been assaulted over the years. Thankfully, with the aid of groups like the Homeschool Legal Defense Association, headed by Michael Farris, the rights and image of home education have been defended.

Another area where critics choose to attack homeschoolers is in saying that homeschooled children receive an unfair advantage against their peers. While that statement is true and factual, it is, amazingly, used in a negative manner. In the 2002 National Geography Bee, ten-year-old Calvin McCarter, homeschooled, won first place. This victory was a great plus for homeschoolers, but an official at the National Geographic organization attacked the McCarter family. The official at National Geographic said that young Calvin McCarter had an unfair advantage over public schoolers, and therefore, it wasn't right for him to win.

Instead of celebrating with the family for their diligence in teaching the boy, she tears them down for obtaining educational excellence and thus beating the peers in public schools. Why any teacher would spurn a well-taught student defies sense.

Nevertheless, on to the bragging.

Academics

Homeschoolers' academic results have greatly outweighed those of their peers in public schools, with homeschooled youngsters claiming high places in the National Geography and Spelling Bees, as well as having a great representation in other academic meets and events across the country.

Besides taking high places in academic meets and events, homeschoolers routinely score much higher in ACT, SAT, and other standardized tests, compared to their peers in public schools. According to the Fraser Institute, a public policy institute based in Canada, homeschoolers score in the 75 to 85 percent range on tests, while public pupils score in the 50s on tests.[9] The average homeschooler in first grade scores 88 percent in reading, 82 in language, and 81 in math. Amazingly, all these scores keep steady and rise as they enter the twelfth grade, except for a lower score on math.[10] But even with the lull in math, they outperform their government school counterparts, huge portions of whom require remedial math in college.

Colleges and universities across the fruited plain have taken note and, in recent history, are avidly hunting out homeschooled teens looking for a place to go to college. Furthermore, more and more colleges and universities have adapted to create a more homeschooling-friendly atmosphere, and other colleges have been created with classes, programs, and an atmosphere specifically tailored toward the home-schooling community.

The simple answer to why public opinion has radically changed on home education is that homeschoolers outperform their peers in government schools and other forms of education. Homeschoolers have been ruling the academic bees for some time now. Year after year, homeschoolers have been in the top placements for the National Geographic

Bee, the Scripps Howard National Spelling Bee, and the USA Math Olympiad.

In addition, you can see severely lower standards in government schools these days. When students have a 3.6 grade point average and score below 20 on the ACT and have to take remedial classes in college, you know we have a problem with standards in schools. However, homeschooled students are making a higher mark on the ACT, scoring an average 23—still higher than public-schooled students.[11] Yet room for improvement is vast.

Family and Discipline

In addition to obvious and documented advantages of homeschooling, perhaps one of the greatest advantages of learning at home is getting to know your family. I know, for certain, that if it weren't for my siblings' and my homeschooled upbringing, we wouldn't know each other as well as we do now. Moreover, homeschooling creates a safe environment for the family to know and learn the dangers of the world and the importance of sticking together and not tearing each other down. You also have a great deal of time that you can spend with other parts of the extended family that most don't have.

On the other hand—and this may seem bad to some my age—homeschooling also provides for healthy discipline to take place. I know my parents never thought twice when using disciplinary action. There were no second thoughts about lawsuits and the like. The teachers—the parents—are allowed to use this discipline when teaching respect, values, and responsibility—something public education is prohibited and inhibited from doing.

Beyond creating a family atmosphere and close family ties, homeschooling also allows for parents to instill religious beliefs and values. The family can teach their own moral values as well as include character curricula in an effort to raise decent human beings. Instead of fearing a lawsuit and the threat of losing the job (as would happen with a teacher in a government school), parents can in the comfort of their home teach their children what they believe in and think.

Homeschooling is not just about results, test scores, and the future business success of a student, but also about time spent the way it should be: with families living their daytime hours together.

Loving Teachers

Above all else, the parents' love and care for their children and students, which are much more than any other person could possibly give, bring them through the hardships and create a motivation to do what it takes to teach and learn. Not that the critics accept this; in fact, they spin it completely the other direction.

The NEA and other such organizations have repeatedly said that most parents do not have the qualifications to successfully teach their children at home—a notion that is completely ridiculous. Parents would not make the sacrifices needed to have a homeschool without loving their children. Therefore, it's easy to see that where their own skills and learning are insufficient, such parents are going to do whatever it takes to successfully teach the children with tutors, curricula, and homeschool cooperatives.

Socialization

As mentioned earlier, along with doubts about the homeschooling atmosphere and educational results, there is large concern over whether homeschoolers are properly socialized. This concern fuels the critics' charge that parents are harming their children because, by being educated at home with a loving parent, they are not learning the necessary socialization skills required in later life—they are insufficiently trained to integrate into society because of their supposed isolation.

You would think, by now, we would be past this issue. I, as a homeschooler, am tired of my intelligence being insulted every time I turn around. Probably the most fabricated or misconstrued idea about homeschooling is that the child is inhibited from obtaining essential socialization skills.

Even after all the successes of homeschooling, the National Education Association still continues to raise this bogey. The NEA's 2000–2001 Resolutions claim that homeschooling cannot provide a comprehensive education experience (i.e., not enough socialization), coupled with other such negative statements.

In a letter to NEA President Bob Chase, the National Home Education Network wrote asking what the resolution regarding home-schooling was based on. He replied, saying, "During the 1998 [Representative Assembly], delegates approved the policy on home-schooling. They were concerned that homeschooled students were not provided a comprehensive education experience because they did not have an opportunity to interact with students of different cultures, economic status or learning styles."[12] In other words, because I stay at home with my mother, brother, and sister—and not several hundred other children down the street—I will fail.

It is obvious that homeschooling has stepped in the way of the NEA's agenda, and because of the fact that homeschoolers make up less than 1 percent of the American population, groups such as the NEA are able to spread this obvious disinformation and deceit.

The premise of the war against homeschooling is that children do not obtain the needed socialization skills. By agreeing with that, you have to concede the point that public schools, private schools, etc., are the only sources for socializing. Ever hear of church, sports, community events, or neighbors down the block? Many home-schoolers, such as myself, play sports, go to church, attend community events, play musical instruments, and do many other things. Maybe if public schools learned from homeschoolers and focused less on socializing in class and focused more on learning, the average test score for public school students might be greater than 50 percent.

The opposition against homeschooling is great but hasn't played out too far in the realm of rhetoric, politics, and propaganda. Yet it has played out in the field of government encroaching on educational freedom. The Homeschool Legal Defense Association has fully documented this.

On the other hand, we have seen statements by politicians and organizations such as the National Education Association that accuse homeschooling of not fully socializing students, with little supporting evidence.

In contrast, dare I suggest that, in proportion, there are more antisocial students in public schools than homeschools. With one-on-one learning action with parents, many homeschoolers are able to communicate far better with adults, compared to their public-schooled peers—leading not to problems in the future but, more likely, greater success in the future. Because of the rough peer pressure (pressure to have sex, use drugs, commit crime, cheat on tests, or pressure to commit other unethical behavior) and social situations, many kids are left out in the cold by other pupils—unlike the alternative choice of homeschooling.

Tied to the antisocial claim is that homeschoolers will most likely fail in later life—a quite humorous claim. Even if you were to concede that homeschooled students are antisocial in grade school, saying that they will fail in later life because of it is nothing short of absurd. Just because people are not part of the "group" in their childhood does not mean they can't communicate in the present or future.

The start of the public education system was in the 1900s, but using the NEA's logic, all those not educated in public schools, including all the Founding Fathers, government officials, doctors, lawyers, and people from all occupations, were not given a comprehensive education experience and not properly socialized.

Most information spread by homeschool critics—including the National Education Association—is nothing short of propaganda in an effort to spread deceit and disinformation. The NEA says that I have not obtained the necessary socialization skills (or communication skills), but I am and I have been communicating information, facts, and my beliefs to you.

Education

In addition, with direct contact with parents, the educating atmosphere and environment is much safer than that of public schools. Coupled with other positive effects and advantages of home education, one of the main points that give homeschoolers a greater advantage over their public-, private-, or charter-schooled peers is the one-on-one teaching between the parent and child. With this interaction, the parent and child get to know each other and have a better and long-lasting relationship. Moreover, this close interaction allows the parent to know the child's strengths and weaknesses.

With the special knowledge that is obtained in a homeschool, parents can create a unique learning curriculum and program specifically designed for the child. Parents as teachers can emphasize certain areas that need more assistance and teach the children in a method that works best. Some children, for example, are very visual learners. With a case of visualization learning, a parent could purchase video curricula, which are readily available in the homeschool market. Still, parents can find other ways of providing a heavily visual learning atmosphere—something that is inhibited in the public school system. This is also true for parents of auditory learners.

The different methods of learning can be adapted to in almost any case, including kinetic learning where the child learns through "doing" and direct involvement. This can be designed together, with the parents and child, to provide a comprehensive education program.

Because of this personal touch, homeschooling can also be very attractive to the parent of a child who requires special education and attention. While public schools do provide special ed programs, it becomes very tiresome and stressful to work with a public school in an effort to provide special education of any real quality. Nobody knows more than a parent the special needs of his or her child. This means a parent can better design an education program specifically for the needs of the child—something that is required when working with children who are slow learners or have other learning problems.

Conclusion

When it comes right down to it, among the many alternatives in education, homeschooling is the best option. It takes on the big boys and surpasses the teaching of private schools, public schools, charter schools, tutors, and almost all other forms of education. This conclusion has many reasons behind it.

First, homeschooling is about as decentralized and unbureaucratic as it can be. Ideas and plans don't have to be run through the school board, looked over and approved by the superintendent, and finally initiated by dozens of teachers. Homeschooling is one-on-one, nonstop action.

Second, homeschooling provides a loving family atmosphere. Although sacrifices have to be made, a family relationship will almost always be retained throughout life. Furthermore, that family environment will always create a safer and more learning-oriented feeling.

Third, homeschooling can almost always provide a greater social interaction between children and adults. With that unique interaction, it will allow a child to be more comfortable among adults and ultimately lead to intelligent communication and interaction.

Fourth, homeschooling provides an opportunity to create a special and unique educational program. That program can be created by picking and choosing curricula, as well as finding audio, video, or kinetic "hands-on" resources. This aspect also can be extremely attractive to a family with a child that requires special education.

In 1985, a Gallup poll surveyed Americans on their opinion of homeschooling. The results might startle a few today because 75 percent of Americans thought homeschooling was a bad idea.[13] Public opinion at that time believed that the notion of parents alone teaching their children at home was a foreign idea, and questions were raised about whether it would or could be successful. However, when homeschoolers had a chance to perform and show the world what results could be realized, public opinion changed drastically. Less than twenty years later, polls show that homeschooling has become much more favorable among citizens.

Some may say I'm biased, and they would be correct in that statement. You see, I have lived the homeschooling life, and in fact, I am still living it. If homeschooling wasn't all that it's cracked up to be and didn't work, I would be out exploring all the negative aspects of homeschooling. I'm just that type of guy. Yet homeschooling does work. Homeschooling has been proved.

Regardless of my opinion on anything to do with education, one thing remains for sure: the love of a parent to his or her children is and will be greater than the love a nonfamily public or private teacher can provide. That main aspect is what will create a motivation to do what it takes to make home education successful.

American parents are becoming aware of what is happening in our schools, and reform has just now begun to take shape. Greater and greater numbers of responsible American parents are taking their children out of government-controlled schools. The only element that has a chance of saving public education is competition between private education and public education. So, charter schools, private schools, and all other forms of education like homeschooling are a key part of our society's paths to education because the best way for education to take place is when the parent has many resources and choices at his or her disposal.

FURTHER READING

Books

- William J. Bennett, Chester E. Finn Jr., and John T. E. Cribb Jr., *The Educated Child: A Parent's Guide from Preschool Through Eighth Grade* (New York: Free Press, 1999).
- Elizabeth Hamilton and Dan Hamilton, *Should I Home School?* (Downers Grove, IL: InterVarsity Press, 1997).

- Christopher J. Klicka, *Home Schooling: The Right Choice* (Sisters, OR: Loyal Publisher, 1998).
- Isabel Lyman, *The Homeschooling Revolution* (Amherst, MA: Bench Press International, 2002).
- Joe Nathan, *Charter Schools: Creating Hope and Opportunity for American Education* (San Francisco, CA: Jossey-Bass, 1996).
- Cynthia Tobias, *The Way They Learn*, a Focus on the Family Book (Wheaton, IL: Tyndale, 1994).

Web Sites
- www.sepschool.org
- www.hslda.org
- www.NHERI.org

Magazines
- *The Teaching Home*
- *Homeschooling Today*

Sound Off

★ MORALITY ★

6

Homosexual Wrongs

In March of 2001, Focus on the Family founder Dr. James Dobson warned that eighteen states were then carrying pro-homosexual legislation, many under the guise of "school safety," "hate crime prevention," "diversity training," and "tolerance."[1]

It cannot be stressed enough that through the current government school system, many groups, including the homosexual lobby, force their agenda onto America's young and unsuspecting people.

This agenda to legitimize homosexuality in mainstream America is not run just through schools but is also attempting to force private organizations to accept them. This invasion into American culture is nothing short of forcing beliefs upon a once-traditional nation.

One individual suggested to me that homosexuals only wish to be accepted in the public eye but would not force themselves into a private group that was unwilling to accept them and/or their lifestyle. But this is not the case. The homosexual community, or at least members of it, has attempted to force its agenda into all aspects of life, such as private groups, churches, schools, and the list goes on. Prime examples of those groups would be the Girl Scouts and Boy Scouts of America.

By way of an awesome "victim" PR campaign and with great help from their tight friends in the media, homosexual groups put pressure on both organizations. The Girl Scouts of America eventually gave in, allowing self-announced homosexuals to become part of their group. However, unlike the Girl Scouts, the Boy Scouts of America resisted. The case went all the way to the Supreme Court.

In the end, it was ruled that the Boy Scouts was a private organization, having the right not to let certain groups into the organization. As a result, Scouts were painted as evil homophobes. Many United Way affiliates, for instance, cut all funds to the Boy Scouts.[2]

Earlier in the book, we examined the many ways intolerant special-interest groups demand tolerance while forcing their ideas into the schools, media, and private organizations. The homosexuality community is much the same.

HOMOSEXUALITY IN THE WORKPLACE

The homosexual community has, expectedly, set its sights on the workplaces of America. In a constant effort to force acceptance and legitimacy, homosexual special-interest groups have advocated legislation that would protect one's sexual orientation against discrimination.

A bill that has been a major threat to traditional values and beliefs is one of the key issues the homosexual community has used to force acceptance, the Employment Non-Discrimination Act (ENDA). The Senate bill (S.1284) is sponsored by none other than the senator from Massachusetts, Teddy Kennedy. The supporters of this bill are, unsurprisingly, key players in the Democratic Party, such as Hillary Clinton, Joseph Lieberman, John Kerry, Tom Daschle, and forty other senators.

The bill would prohibit discrimination against homosexuals and officially make homosexuality a right, protected along with race, religion, ethnicity, national origin, sex, and disability against discrimination by federally funded lawsuits. Supporters of ENDA say that the legislation is necessary to end widespread discrimination against homosexuals and transsexuals. "It extends fair-employment practices, not special rights, to lesbians, to gay men, to bisexuals," says Senator Clinton.[3]

I find this very disturbing.

Say I own a family-run business and I wish to have a family-type atmosphere. I don't want someone with that type of lifestyle around my family or me, and the government has no right to make me.

This bill shows the true colors of those in Congress. It exposes their obvious untraditional marriage beliefs and antifamily values. Homosexuals choose to be that way. Homosexuality is a behavior—not something they are born with, such as race. The fact is, gays and lesbians have claimed an illegitimate minority status, which is endorsed by many on the Left.

If I were a member of the legitimate minority group that homosexuals may be joining, I would be outraged. For a certain group of people to be awarded the same rights as me, just because of a behavior, is odious.

Senator Kennedy has been quoted as saying, "We must continue the progress toward freeing ourselves from this form of discrimination. America will never be America until we do."[4]

With this legislation, legal action can be taken against those who discriminate against homosexuals, true enough, but only at the expense of free thought, free speech, freedom of religion, and the freedom of an individual's own conscience and convictions. It stems from extreme intolerance. They insist that you be tolerant of everything they do, but they are intolerant of everything you do. They can dish it out, but can't take it. The government wants to force me to be tolerant, but homosexuals don't have to be.

Look what happened to radio talk show host Dr. Laura Schlessinger. Because of her stance on homosexuality, gays and lesbians did everything they could to protest her television program and boycotted advertisers. Their actions resulted in her show getting pulled.

The bill does include exemptions for religious organizations, but is deceptive in that most experts and legislators believe, at the time of this writing, that the courts will strike it down.

I belong to a small church in a rural community. Sometime ago, we were looking for a new youth pastor and found one. However, if a homosexual applied for that position and was turned down, with this legislation and exemption overturned, our church could come under fire with a federally funded lawsuit. Our small church would have a very hard time surviving if the exemption were struck down. Because of the fact that it is impossible to fully prove that someone was discriminated against based on sexual orientation, many religious institutions and organizations could possibly come under fire because of ENDA.

This example is another tactic of the homosexual community that will expand federal power over the workplace, and by threatening the private sector with federally funded lawsuits, it will frighten more and more employers from being selective while choosing employees.

HOMOSEXUALITY IN PUBLIC EDUCATION

Those who control what is taught in public schools control the future culture of the nation. The homosexual community, which is a tiny fraction of Americans, realizes that.

Under the banner of "hate crime" prevention, groups such as Planned Parenthood travel to schools around the country to teach young students about, among other things, homosexuality and homophobia.

However, it goes much farther than that. Homosexuality is not only taught in public schools, but it is portrayed as an acceptable lifestyle and act, and those who believe it is a sin as homophobic hate-mongers.

One example would be at a high school in California. Planned Parenthood was invited and, without parental consent, proceeded to speak about sexual education. The freshman health class was instructed to form a human circle and then was asked questions such as, "Does your religion believe against or think homosexuality is a sin or something wrong?"[5] The obvious repercussions for those stepping in the circle were peer pressure and embarrassment.

This is just one example of that which happens in "health" classes across the country. Still, many insist that we must continue to have this sort of education in order to prevent hate crimes and homophobia among the youth of America. The NEA obviously holds this position, because in the 2001–2002 National Education Association Resolutions, they promoted "multiculture" education in an effort to reduce "racism, homophobia, and all other forms of prejudice, and discrimination."[6]

The homosexual community, having anecdotal evidence to support its claim to widespread homophobia, lobbies hard for legislation that teaches homosexuality in public schools. In the National Education Association's own reports, they show in their notes that much of the evidence used to push for "hate crime prevention" programs is merely based on anecdotal evidence.

When a community of like-minded groups forms an alliance and prevents those from the other side to have free speech in the debate, you know there is a problem. Yet that is exactly what the homosexual community has done.

In a board meeting in February 2002, the NEA directors approved the report of the NEA Task Force on Sexual Orientation. The report says that gay, lesbian, bisexual, and transgendered (lumped together as "g/l/b/t" in the report) public school students face discrimination, harassment, and abuse on a daily basis but gives no source for backing it up.

The report basically concludes that there is a major problem in public education for these students, and programs must be implemented to solve the problem. However, the task force is even ignorant of those who may be homosexuals, saying, "Although precise figures are not available, there can be no question that the number of g/l/b/t students is significant. The most reliable research on this issue shows that between five and six percent of American students are gay, lesbian, or bisexual."

Their source? It reads,

The most recent and comprehensive study of adolescent youth in the United States is the National Longitudinal Study of Adolescent Health, undertaken by the Carolina Population Center at the University of

North Carolina Chapel Hill. That study surveyed a nationally representative sample of more than 12,000 7th to 12th grade students and found that 6 percent of participants reported that they felt same-sex romantic attraction.[7]

Do you see something wrong with this picture? The largest teachers union in America is lobbying to teach homosexuality in public schools based on a survey of students who say that they have had a same-sex romantic attraction at one point in time. Having merely a boy-to-boy or girl-to-girl attraction does not necessarily mean someone is homosexual, much the same way that an attraction to the opposite sex does not mean you have had sex. And they say there is no homosexual agenda. If there weren't, they wouldn't be pulling these kinds of shenanigans.

The so-called hate crime prevention in schools, by way of teaching homosexuality, is a farce and just another way to force their agenda into the open. Under the name of "tolerance, school safety, multiculturalism, etc.," they are successfully teaching that the homosexual lifestyle is acceptable!

In California, for instance, there was legislation passed recently that requires the teaching of homosexuality in public schools. From kindergarten to twelfth grade, students are taught the acceptance of homosexuality. Also, students are being taught a moral equivalency between heterosexuality and homosexuality.[8]

Although there is no hard evidence suggesting that homosexuals are constantly being attacked verbally and physically, we could even concede that point. But then flip it around and you'll still see where the bias lies: let us imagine that there was a widespread prejudice toward Christianity. In order to combat that, the public school system officials wouldn't even think of teaching the history of Christianity and explaining that Christianity is a great and acceptable lifestyle and religion. However, school administrators and teachers would probably treat each discrimination case independently and use disciplinary action, if necessary. That's exactly what happened when anti-Semitism and discrimination against blacks were widespread.

Therefore, knowing that, we can see that in order to put a stop to homophobia, we don't have to teach it; schools just have to deal with each case and use discipline.

As pointed out in Chapter 4, if the word *religion* were behind the homosexual lifestyle, there would be a huge public outcry, forcing the prohibition of homosexuality in public schools. However, there is no public outcry because homosexuality is not a religion, though it is objectionable to many parents around the country.

Although on the surface, homosexuality couldn't seem to be compared with religion, as with religion, homosexuality is a lifestyle. It is a subject for which many demand respect and tolerance. Homosexuality is a mind-set and lifestyle that Christian, heterosexual parents wouldn't want taught to their children, but fundamental Christianity is a mind-set and lifestyle that homosexual parents wouldn't want taught to their kids.

But rather than see it as a conflict in life views, in which people are bound to have differences—even strident ones—homosexuals actively work to force their view on others.

I will tell anyone that I believe homosexuality is a sin and a disgusting lifestyle. However, instead of attacking my argument, I am personally attacked by many in the homosexual community. I have received hundreds of e-mails informing me that I am a "homophobe" and full of "prejudice." The problem is, a "homophobe" is a person that is discriminatory toward homosexuals. Moreover, according to my *Webster's*, someone who is *prejudiced* is defined as a person who has "an irrational attitude of hostility directed against an individual."

Stating that homosexuality is evil and disgusting is not equal to saying that a homosexual is evil and disgusting—which brings up the relevance of comparing religion with homosexuality.

I will tell you that I believe the teaching of Jehovah's Witnesses is false teaching and goes against my Christian beliefs. However, I'm not saying that those who believe in that religion are the scum of the earth and deserve nothing but death—nothing even remotely close to that. I have no problem with their religion, even though it contradicts my own. In fact, I have known and met Jehovah's Witnesses before and had nothing against them. Being a Christian, I believe that the religion of Judaism is no longer true and therefore a false teaching. However, I have great respect for many Jewish talk show hosts, leaders, pundits, and those from all walks of life. Disagreeing with one's political party, religion, or moral lifestyle doesn't mean you condemn someone personally.

Using this logic, you can see that many in the homosexual community will not step up to the plate and debate the issues; instead, many lower themselves to uncalled for personal attacks.

ARGUING AGAINST THE GAY "GENE" THEORY

Perhaps the greatest case for the acceptance of homosexuality is the farce of the gay gene.

Many homosexuals parade around stating that homosexuality is a genetic trait and something people are born with. Self-announced homosexual and activist Rosie O'Donnell submitted this evidence: "Every animal kingdom and every species, 10 percent of the population is homosexual."[9] Ms. O'Donnell left out the evidence to back up this statement but, in doing that, did the same thing many homosexual activists do—which is spread lies and disinformation to further their cause.

However, does the case of whether homosexuality is a choice or not really matter? The Human Rights Campaign, a homosexual activist group, doesn't think so. "The vast majority of gay people will tell you that same-sex orientation is an innate part of who you are and is not changeable," a spokesman said. "But in the final analysis, it really shouldn't matter."[10]

Whether the sincerity of that statement is valid or not, the simple fact is that whether homosexuality is a genetic trait or not does matter.

If homosexuality is genetic and not a choice, then the lifestyle and act must be accepted by everyone because it cannot be prevented. However, if it is a choice, then anyone has the right to name homosexuality unacceptable and immoral, based on their code of ethics. (We are all postmoderns here, aren't we?)

The scientific basis that the homosexual community uses to prove the gay gene theory is two different studies conducted in 1993 and 1995. The studies found a specific marker in the X chromosome that links homosexuality in men.

In 1993, biologist Dean Hamer of the National Cancer Institute found that in 40 pairs of gay brothers, 33 of them had the same set of DNA sequences in a part of the chromosome called Xq28. This has called for many homosexual leaders to submit this evidence and demand respect and acceptance of homosexuality because of this apparent genetic trait. However, in late June of 1995, reports were confirmed that Dean Hamer was being investigated by the Office of Research Integrity at the Department of Health and Human Services. Reports found that Hamer may have selectively reported his research and data—which has led many to question the credibility of his research.[11]

Furthermore, in the late 1990s, a team of researchers at the University of Western Ontario in Canada found no trace or evidence of the gay gene in homosexual men. The study found that the region of the X chromosome known as Xq28 has nothing to do with the sexual "orientation" of a person.[12]

Neurologist George Rice of the university studied the DNA of 52 pairs of gay brothers and found that their Xq28 sequences were no more similar than what might happen from sheer chance.

Despite the debunking of evidence to back the gay gene theory, homosexual advocates continue to use this outdated evidence to prove the existence of a homosexual genetic trait.

Still, there is even more evidence that suggests homosexuality is not a trait that a person is born with. Identical twins, for instance, share the same set of chromosomal patterns. Therefore, if one twin's DNA has a homosexual genetic trait, then it is inevitable that both twins will be homosexuals. However, that is not the case with all twins. When one twin is homosexual, the probability of the other identical twin being homosexual is 50 percent. However, that can be attributed to environmental experience, because twins spend more time together than with anyone else.[13]

Thus, the gay gene theory is, once again, debunked by using logical scientific research.

In addition, there is even more evidence against homosexual genes. If homosexuality is, indeed, despite this evidence, a genetic trait, that gene would eventually be ousted from the gene pool because homosexuals tend not to reproduce. Instead, homosexuality has appeared in civilizations across time; while one culture may have homosexuality, others don't. In some parts of the world, homosexuality flourishes; in other parts of the world, homosexuality is not present.

Also, if homosexuality is a genetic trait, it would be next to impossible to change the lifestyle from homosexuality to heterosexuality. However, it is not impossible to change sexual orientations.

In the June 2002 issue of the American Psychologists Association journal *Professional Psychology: Research and Practice*, Dr. Warren Throckmorton has written an article titled "Initial Empirical and Clinical Findings Concerning the Change Process for Ex-Gays." The research presented caused a stir among the psychology world. The article finds that sexual orientation can be changed. "[The research] suggests that sexual orientation, once thought to be an unchanging sexual trait, is actually quite flexible for many people, changing as a result of therapy for some, ministry for others and spontaneously for still others," Dr. Throckmorton said.[14]

Furthermore, the report went on to say that the change from homosexuality to heterosexuality is very helpful and positive to the majority of those who experience the change.

There have been many religious groups that specialize in the helping of homosexuals to "come out" of their lifestyle. Stephen Bennett

Ministries, for instance, does this sort of thing and has had great success. Former homosexual Stephen Bennett, who became a Christian and "came out" of that lifestyle, founded this ministry. While the overall goal is to share the gospel of Jesus Christ, Bennett focuses on reaching those who are homosexuals. Being a songwriter, artist, speaker, writer, and now a representative for Concerned Women for America, Stephen Bennett has a great outlet to work with, and he has been successfully getting their message out for some time now.

Another organization is Exodus International. This ministry is specifically dedicated to bringing people out of the gay and lesbian lifestyle through the teaching of Christianity. In an effort to do that, they work as a referral service for those looking for freedom from homosexuality and find counseling and ministry centers. This organization has over two hundred affiliates nationwide that help in this cause to reform homosexuals in the depressing lifestyle.

Yes, change is possible. This has been evident not only through psychological reports, but also through the success of religious (mainly Christian) organizations.

With this incredible load of evidence mounting up against the gay gene theory, it would be a safe assumption to say that homosexuality is actually not something you are born with but a sovereign choice.

CHRISTIANS AND ATHEISTS

For Christians and Jews, the answer is simple. The Old Testament calls homosexuality an "abomination" or "detestable." Leviticus 18:22 says, "Do not lie with a man as one lies with a woman; that is detestable." It later goes on to say, "If a man lies with a man as one lies with a woman, both of them have done what is detestable" (20:13).

Clearly, God does not look positively upon homosexuality, but looks upon it with disgust. However, what do the New Testament and Jesus have to say about homosexuality? First Corinthians 6:9–10 says, "Do you not know that the wicked will not inherit the kingdom of God? Do not be deceived: Neither the sexually immoral nor idolaters nor adulterers nor male prostitutes nor homosexual offenders nor thieves nor the greedy nor drunkards nor slanderers nor swindlers will inherit the kingdom of God."

Jesus said, "Haven't you read, that at the beginning the Creator 'made them male and female,' and said, 'For this reason a man will leave his father and mother and be united to his wife, and the two will become one flesh'? So they are no longer two, but one. Therefore what God has joined together, let man not separate" (Matt. 19:4–6).

For atheists, the answer is very simple in regard to this issue. With no God to shape a moral code, it's pretty much up to the feelings of the individual, and many find homosexuality a disgusting lifestyle and choose to be "homophobes."

Furthermore, the goal of many atheists is, arguably, to work to bring humanity to the greatest form it can be—this is certainly true for the rigorously humanistic ones. However, since it is totally impossible for homosexuals to reproduce, you can then assume that homosexuality is counterproductive to the evolution of society.

In addition, being an atheist, morality can't "hold" you down from having a "good time," so why let the homosexual lifestyle throw a wet blanket on it? If you speak to a homosexual and study the accounts of current and former homosexuals, there is no doubt that the life is depressing.

HEALTH AND SEXUAL ABUSE

Ponder this: by at least one estimate, a third of all the Girl Scout counselors are lesbians, and the Patriots' Trail Girl Scout Council in Massachusetts has initiated a lesbian "mentoring" program. This may sound all well and good on the surface to some, but reports show an increase in sexual molestations.[15]

As of July 2002, Big Brothers Big Sisters of America (BBBSA) requires that all five hundred of its local affiliates include homosexuals as volunteers and mentors to children. Moreover, many parents would be surprised to know that their child could be paired up with a gay or lesbian mentor without their knowledge.[16] The majority of children mentored by this organization come from single-parent homes, with boys who are fatherless. When that boy who is desperate for male attention is paired up with a gay man, you tell me what the results could be.

Entertain those thoughts and be speculative if you like, but evidence suggests that the majority of male homosexuals have an attraction to young boys. A study in the *Archives of Sexual Behavior*, with gay researchers Karla Jay and Allen Young, reports that 73 percent of gay men they surveyed engaged in sex with boys sixteen to nineteen years of age and sometimes younger.[17]

An additional study of 229 convicted child molesters found that 86 percent of those surveyed identified themselves as homosexual or bisexual.[18] While certainly not all homosexuals are pedophiles, this causes concern for the well-being of impressionable children.

America's children are at risk. There is no doubt about it.

In addition to molestations and the risk of harm to America's children, there are other health problems associated with the "activities" of homosexuals and their lifestyles. For those who are homosexuals, for example, life expectancy decreases by thirty years.[19] That's a major decrease in years of one's life!

Furthermore, numerous sexually transmitted diseases (STDs) can be obtained by continuing that lifestyle. The essence of homosexuality goes against the continuation of life and has the power of destroying it with STDs. The responsibility for the explosion of the AIDS and HIV viruses can be laid on the homosexual lifestyle. When a homosexual has hundreds of anonymous "partners" throughout his life, why has the spread of AIDS been a shock to the world?

SOME FRIENDLY ADVICE

Here are some tips for homosexuals to consider if they wish to reasonably and logically debate on a wide scale with Christian conservatives such as myself:

First, get the bed off the front porch. Sure, sex is an issue in a hetero-sexual's life, but the issue is usually not something that is paraded around and shoved in the faces of other people. Although our society is becoming more and more immoral and the talk of this issue is more openly discussed, it is not widely accepted as a topic of discussion and is definitely not something most people want to be confronted with.

Second, don't force your lifestyle on people who don't want it. I don't want to outlaw homosexuality, and I don't want to make demons out of homosexuals, but the more and more the homosexual community forces this type of acceptance of their lifestyle onto traditional Americans, the more gays and lesbians are going to be hated and not accepted by many.

Third, the homosexualizing of children in public schools is going to be firmly resisted by many parents. This has much to do with forced acceptance of a lifestyle, and not a single person I know wants to be forced to do something—especially teens and other young people.

Last, be friendly. I realize this sounds naive, but the homosexual community is one of the most hostile groups in the entire political landscape of America. In order to get your point across, you don't dismiss someone's argument and demonize him or her. The campaign of homosexuality is one of attacking the opponent and not offering its own ideas and opinions.

These suggestions, I know, will be immediately scoffed at, dismissed, and thrown away by anyone having to do with the politics of homosexuality. The key philosophy behind these tips is the idea that you have to show respect to get respect, and you have to be civil in order for your opponents to be open to debate. I'm not holding my breath for these people.

CONCLUSION

Yeah, yeah, I know, I am an intolerant kid who has been brainwashed by his parents, is regurgitating what his dad tells him, and is a poster boy for the failures of homeschooling and conservatism. I've heard it a million times. Even with my good intentions of my opinion regarding the issue of homosexuality, I will be sacrificed upon the altar of tolerance by many in this vicious community. I predict the future attacks on my opinions.

Not that any of that bothers me, mind you, but it just reiterates what you just read. Homosexual politics is typically vicious, and its practitioners will stop at nothing to have their opinions and lifestyle accepted by America.

Bill O'Reilly can call people with my point of view "holy roller[s],"[20] culture can mock the traditional viewpoint, and the mainstream media can compare this view to that of the Taliban. At the point when someone is attacked fervently and prevented from giving an opinion for fear of response, the idea of free speech is lost.

Because the current state of the homosexual agenda is on that course of the destruction of American principles, it must be resisted. That road is tough, your resolve is required to be strong, your principles must not be compromised, and the attacks are vicious.

Foremost, holding your resolve is the greatest thing you can do. However, it requires a deep guarding of beliefs and a regular reaffirming of beliefs. It may become attractive and reasonable to give up and become a moderate on this issue. Still, tolerance is nothing short of the acceptance of immorality, and moderation is the virtue of those with no convictions.

Second, those who control words control culture. Therefore, guarding your moral compass is necessary because words and analogies can be twisted and formed into a case that appears to be logical, but is simply propaganda.

In addition, bringing common sense back into the issue of homosexuality is needed. At times, we get so caught up in debates, issues, and statements that simple common sense is unintentionally left at the door. Yet in reaffirming beliefs and reevaluating a moral point, it must be brought back. That the very issue of whether homosexuality is a choice or not is really an issue just shows that common sense is nearly gone. Why? Because the act that makes someone a homosexual is a choice in and of itself.

As a Christian, I believe homosexuality is a sin and is evil. However, my faith teaches me to hate the sin but love the sinner. Although I don't hate homosexuals, I hate the practice of homosexuality, and I don't wish to be forced to accept it. If, later in life, I own a small business, I don't want to be forced to work with any homosexual that comes along, and the government has no right whatsoever to force me.

Intolerance is negative only in relation to what it is associated. Intolerance against the current agenda of the homosexual community is not a negative thing. However, as the battle drums continue, the shouts of "intolerance" will continue without the notice of their own hatred.

FURTHER READING

Books

- Bob Davies and Lori Rentzel, *Coming Out of Homosexuality* (Downers Grove, IL: InterVarsity Press, 1994).

- Joseph Nicolosi and Linda Ames Nicolosi, *A Parent's Guide to Preventing Homosexuality* (Downers Grove, IL: InterVarsity Press, 2002).

- Jeffrey Satinover, M.D., *Homosexuality and the Politics of Truth* (Grand Rapids, MI: Baker Books, 1999).

Web Sites

- www.sbministries.org
- www.exodusnorthamerica.org

7

Abortion: The American Holocaust

ABORTION IS DEFINED AS THE "SPONTANEOUS OR artificially induced expulsion of an embryo or fetus."[1] The concept is easy enough to grasp, yet this widely known term points to a very difficult issue. With little examination, there are clear-cut answers to many questions, true. But the fight over abortion in America is different from just your average, kitchen-table debate.

Part of the problem is that there is little actual communication on the issue. Instead, both sides tend to talk past each other and regularly fire propaganda over the bow of the media. The pro-abortionists say that a woman has a constitutional right to do what she wishes with her body, as the fetus is only potential life and part of her body. The pro-lifers say that the fetus is really a live, human baby, and to abort it would be no less than to murder a one-year-old toddler.

It's an endless stream of public relations campaigns from both sides. The pro-life side appeals to one's sense of morality by showing how barbaric the abortion procedure is and how it affects the lives of those who go through such trauma. On the other side, pro-abortionists show pictures of bombed abortion centers and the mistakes made by pro-lifers.

The ideas and defense of the abortion community in America were basically written by Supreme Court Justice Harry Blackmun during the case of *Roe* v. *Wade*. Throughout the entire court opinion, the words *potential life* are written. This has been the battle cry of the National Organization for Women and other feminist groups.

Personally, my earliest memories on this subject are always surrounded by emotion. Abortion, an "operation" on an unborn child, has been discussed around me from my earliest days either by my parents or on Christian talk radio. The secular media always had a few things to say on the debate as well. When other subjects are discussed, often the reactions hover around general disinterest, depending on the audience and their stake in the subject. But abortion, universally, polarizes. There is no middle ground. Either a person favors the violent end to an unborn life or not. No room in between.

That's where the debate gets bitter. A poll conducted after the 2000 elections showed the abortion debate divided. This divide and disagreement make sense in a nation drifting with little sense of itself; abortion is a fundamental issue in what makes an American. Sure, you can say that it's a tough issue and must be carefully considered, but at the end of the day, you are either for one side or another.

Why is there such a divide? Not only because of the fact that there are just two choices, but because you are choosing between two distinct viewpoints of what the operation of abortion really is. Is abortion the disposal of tissue growing in a woman's body, merely potential life—or is abortion the murder and destruction of sacred, human life? Therein lies the debate.

ABORTION: A CONCLUSION

So, here are the choices: I can side with the likes of the National Organization for Women, Planned Parenthood, the Democratic National Committee, and the political powers of the left-wing agenda. On the other hand, I can side with Concerned Women for America, Focus on the Family, Operation Rescue National, and the right-wing side of the political issue.

The liberal, pro-choice side argues that women have the right to do what they wish with their bodies, as it is a constitutional right, based on the Supreme Court decision in the case of *Roe* v. *Wade* in 1973. The conservative, pro-life side argues that once life begins in the womb, it is sacred and protected by the same laws that make it illegal to murder a man on the street. Both victims are human lives; the only difference is the place of death. They champion the ideas of morality, justice, and the documents that shaped our great nation.

One side is based on an ideology that cannot be compromised, seeking a better life for everyone. The other side in the issue plays politics and distortion in order to gain an agenda of power. You can take your pick of who's who. Or, on second thought, I'll do the thinking for you. The politicos who distort, lie, and push immoral values in order to force an agenda of murder are in the camp of the National Organization for Women, Planned Parenthood, and the American Civil Liberties Union.

The right to have an abortion is based on the so-called right to privacy. This has two conditions. One, that the Constitution protects the right of "privacy," and two, that the privacy of a mother includes the unborn baby child. That's the sticking point.

In order to make a case against abortion, we must first set up the playing field of definitions. First, you must agree that murder is wrong and immoral. After that, you must define what a human is. My *Webster's* defines a *human* as a "bipedal primate mammal (Homo sapiens); any living or extinct member of the family to which the primate belongs."

So, is a fetus included in that? Clearly, yes.

A child developing in the womb is still human—no matter what stage of development he might be at. He's not a pear, a donkey, or an appendix until the moment he's born. From conception, the child is an individual human, separate from his mother in identity. The baby has his own DNA and separate bloodstream. In fact, if the baby's Rh factor deviates from the mother's and that blood mixes, it can cause a rejection, resulting in complications or death.[2] This shows that the fetus is separate, not like an organ in a woman's body.

As murder hangs on the distinction of life, the question of when life really begins is key to the abortion debate. Killing something that isn't alive—even if it's human—isn't murder. From what I see, life begins at conception. Where else could it start? Some say at the first beat of the heart. Still others believe at birth. Since the baby possesses a separate identity from the mother at conception, I propose to you that life begins then. This makes taking the life of the embryo murder.

The main difference between an embryo and you is your developmental stage. Tied to this is the level of dependency. An embryo completely depends on the mother to live, as it does throughout almost the entire pregnancy. Yet I depend on my parents and family for protection, food, clothing, and all the necessities of life. Using the logic of NOW and Planned Parenthood, parents should be able to "abort" the life of even the *born* child that depends on them. To see where this thinking can lead, bioethicist Peter Singer has argued for the merits of parents being able to kill "defective" infants because of the dependence of the child being too much of a burden to parents.[3] Even making it out alive is no guarantee that innocent life will not be snuffed out by those on whom it's dependent.

Abortion is completely, thoroughly, and always murder, unless done to prevent the death of the mother. No, I did not include rape. I don't understand the logic in punishing the unborn baby for the bad thing that happened to the mother.

According to a study released by the Alan Guttmacher Institute (AGI), from the time of the passage of *Roe* v. *Wade* in 1973, to 1998, over 38 million babies have been aborted.[4] There have been no recent studies released on the number of abortions as of the time of this writing; however, based on data by AGI, many estimate the number at approximately 42 million.

By comparison, Hitler murdered 12 million, and Stalin, 20 million.

In the realm of holocaust, we have managed to lead the modern world in sheer atrocity.

It is not only the senseless destruction of lives that are all potential and no realization that is at issue here. In addition, there is the culture that these murders create, a culture that holds life to be irrelevant if inconvenient.

If a society in its right mind can stand up and say that killing unborn babies is right, what comes next? Perhaps taking a page from Peter Singer, my father has sarcastically suggested that we should completely outlaw abortion, but should allow parents the right to murder their children up to the age of three. That way they would at least have to face their children before making the decision to take their lives. A form of renting children to see if they'll do.

However, in all seriousness, he has a point. Based on the strain of abortion thought, I propose that we, as Americans, allow for parents to kill their children up to the age of three years old and for the option of children to kill their parents once they are past the age of seventy-five.

Additionally, we could push for such killing as a powerful population-control tool in our nation. From there, ask this: Why not also gun down anyone who attempts to enter our country illegally? How about handing out the death penalty to anyone who commits a crime?

Does this sound like rational thought? Well, it is a logical step in the "advancement" of our ideals, morals, and beliefs in the nation of "freedom." This may be a barbaric idea to the countries of the world and maybe even some people in this country, but if we intend to have any logic in our beliefs, they must line up.

The insane statements above go into the direct line of abortion thought. If you can deface and destroy one of the few things sacred on this earth—life—anything can be rationalized as moral and just. If we, as a nation, can decide that it is right, moral, and just to murder the essence of innocence and helplessness, then we must hang our heads in shame and repent, or let us be damned.

Our society and culture cannot, on the one hand, cry crocodile tears for the perceived injustice against homosexuals as an example and, on the other, willingly allow lives to be sacrificed by the millions.

Thomas Jefferson said, "The chief purpose of the government is to protect life. Abandon that and you have abandoned all."

Even the founding document on which our nation was supposed to be based, the Declaration of Independence, says that "we"—the nation—hold these truths to be self-evident: that we are endowed by God with certain inalienable rights, and among these are life, liberty, and the pursuit of happiness. All these inalienable rights tend to contradict what is considered law in our "free" republic.

The American government has recently ruled that for purposes of health care coverage, an unborn fetus shall legally be considered a life. At the same time, we continue to rule that for purposes of abortion, that same unborn fetus is not a life. How long can we continue to hold these two opposites together?

In the midst of this horrendous slaughter, there is a subset of horror called partial birth abortion. We legally allow so-called physicians to birth a child so that all parts of this living and breathing human being are delivered, only to end the child's life by penetrating the skull and evacuating the brain into a suction machine. What monumental hypocrisy we exhibit to the world and ourselves when we claim to care about injustice here and abroad while favoring and protecting such barbarism.

The Planned Parenthood Federation of America and other special-interest groups combined to create a specific agenda to "educate" our children in the enlightened philosophy of abortion and sexual liberty. It may surprise some readers that our schools allow such free access to the children of this country by such insidious special interests, but that access cannot be realistically denied. Any attempt to stanch the flow of propaganda pouring into our schools is labeled "intolerance" and "ignorance," and the ridicule and loss of professional status among peers effectively stifle any protests against this systematic, ongoing indoctrination.

It's a power that cannot be reckoned with. It has a power on our educational institutions, it has a power on our news media, it has a power on our entertainment industry, and it has a power on the legislative bodies that run this country. Funding this power are the tax dollars of Americans and an endless flow of political donations.

The only thing it does not have its claws in is the American people. We can decide what we want. Thus, we have to decide on the issue of abortion and work to return our nation to morality.

ABORTION: THE OPERATION

The actual operation procedure for abortion has got to be one of the most barbaric and disheartening medical operations in the world. Although you can find public video of many of the operations performed in the United States, it is unheard of to find video of an abortion procedure.

Why is that? Well, it is obvious that those who want abortion really don't want to delve into the essence of what it is. It is unarguably murder of innocent life, and to see the body of a tiny little baby being murdered is too much for those who champion the "pro-choice" position.

There are many forms of abortion operations, depending on the stage of the pregnancy and other circumstances. Suction aspiration is one, as described by the National Right to Life organization,

> Suction aspiration, or "vacuum curettage," is the abortion technique used in most first trimester abortions. A powerful suction tube with a sharp cutting edge is inserted into the womb through the dilated cervix. The suction dismembers the body of the developing baby and tears the placenta from the wall of the uterus, sucking blood, amniotic fluid, placental tissue, and fetal parts into a collection bottle.[5]

Another form of abortion, performed in the first trimester, is dilation and curettage. In this technique, a curved blade is placed into the womb, and the body of the baby is cut into pieces and then removed.

Salt poisoning is another form of abortion that is used during the second and third trimesters. A needle is inserted through the mother's abdomen, and amniotic fluid is withdrawn and then replaced with a liquid of concentrated salt. The baby breathes in, swallowing the salt, and is poisoned. The chemical solution causes pain, burning, and deterioration of the baby's skin. After an hour, the child dies. The mother goes into labor about thirty hours after the murder and delivers a dead and burned baby.

The graphic procedure of abortion is a nightmarish form of legalized murder, for whatever rationalized reason.

ABORTION: LIFE AFTER DEATH

The aftereffects to a woman following an abortion are undoubtedly negative. Not only does guilt often set in, but abortion may also lead to medical complications in the would-be mother, higher chance of suicide, and higher chance of getting breast cancer.[6]

While it may be considered a view of life after death—that is, life after abortion—it may be more properly described as death after death, for some. The mortality rate of those who have had abortions is amazingly higher than those who completed their pregnancy and gave birth.

There is a definite effect that abortion brings to a woman. That effect cannot be ignored, as it not only creates severe guilt, depression, and regret, but has also been known to sharply decrease the quality of life for the would-be mother. Many women relive the abortion experience in their minds each year on the anniversary date. With the anticipation of the coming date they are likely to experience depression, suicidal thoughts, headaches, nightmares, difficulty concentrating, or a deep sadness. Mother's Day can become a difficult day to deal with and can become a trigger to the traumatic memories.

The birth of a baby can trigger a post-traumatic reaction. Or even the sight of a newborn can cause distress, and the memories return to the abortion. Grief, denial, distress. It's all about life after abortion.

Additionally, such feelings can come to the father of the aborted baby. Some cases have turned into long court debates on whether the mother should be able to abort the baby without any say from the father.

On its Web site, Planned Parenthood has frequently asked questions regarding abortion, with one asking, "What will I feel after an abortion?" Their answer? "Most women feel relief. Sudden hormonal changes after abortion can make you feel anger, regret, guilt, or sadness for a little while."[7]

I wonder, since when has a conscience been explained away as temporary "hormonal" changes? Maybe they can develop medicine that destroys all emotional reactions to immorality.

Planned Parenthood has set an agenda to hide the obvious medical complications as a result of an abortion procedure. Charlotte Taft, a counselor and director of a Dallas abortion clinic, was counseling women prior to their abortion operation concerning the mental anxiety that would follow. She attempted to prepare women with the tough issues that come along with an abortion. Knowing the information Taft gave her clients, some chose not to go through with an abortion.

Planned Parenthood criticized Taft, refusing to send referrals to her clinic. The president of Planned Parenthood of Dallas and Northeast Texas scolded her, taking exception to the statements made by Ms. Taft about the pro-choice community not being completely honest with women.

However, nothing can explain away not only the emotional baggage that is carried through life as a result of an abortion, but also the health risks of breast cancer, higher statistical chances of suicide, and other health dangers.

As for emotional and mental problems, they tend to be very long term, according to reports.[8] As a woman approaches the anniversary date of her abortion or passes by the abortion clinic, it's a reminder of what happened and brings back the guilt and regret associated with aborting the pregnancy.

According to a study done by STAKES, the statistical analysis unit of Finland's National Research and Development Center for Welfare and Health, the risk of death from suicide within a year of an abortion was more than seven times higher than the risk of suicide within a year of childbirth.[9] Abortion is clearly linked to a high increase in suicide risk. This important finding has been conducted by interview-based studies in which 30 to 55 percent have consistently shown extremely high levels of suicidal ideation and reports of suicide attempts among women who have had an abortion.[10]

Physically, the results are still no better. In addition to suicide, the risks take an even greater turn with the risk of breast cancer sharply rising to double. The same Finland researchers also reported that those who have had abortions are four times more likely to die prematurely than if they gave birth.[11] Evidence also suggests that it rises even more with further abortions.[12]

There is also more evidence that shows the dangers of abortion in relation to breast cancer. A study of nearly 2,000 women that appeared in the *Journal of the National Cancer Institute* in 1994 found that women having abortions increased their risk of getting breast cancer by 50 percent.[13] The study gets even scarier for women under the age of eighteen. For a teen with no previous pregnancies, having an abortion after the eighth week of pregnancy increased the risk of breast cancer to even higher than that for older women. Women with a family history of breast cancer fared even worse.

What does Planned Parenthood say about this? On its Web site, it answers the question of whether abortion causes breast cancer: "No. But abortion does not offer the same protection against breast cancer as a full term pregnancy. Hundreds of so-called 'crisis pregnancy centers' scare women about abortion. They lie about the medical and emotional effects of abortion."[14] There couldn't be some sort of agenda behind that, could there?

Despite what the pro-abortionists say, there is definite and specific evidence that suggests emotional and physical problems occur as a result of abortion. There is no denying it.

However, these physical complications do not always come after an abortion but during the abortion. Although doctors use local anesthesia for an abortion, 97 percent of women having abortions reported experiencing pain during the procedure.[15] A third of those surveyed described the pain as "intense." Additionally, a third described the pain as "severe" or "very severe."[16] Compared to other pains, researchers have rated the pain from abortion as more painful than a bone fracture, about the same as cancer pain, though not as painful as an amputation.[17]

All this evidence shows that abortion comes not only with emotional and psychological problems, but also with physical problems, and many other complications that harm families and futures.

WHAT CAN I DO?

If you've made it this far and agree that murdering an unborn, innocent baby is immoral, you'll probably be left with the question of, What do we do now?

In his book *Letters to a Young Conservative*, Dinesh D'Souza hits the nail on the head about the pro-life movement: "In my view, the pro-life movement at this point should focus on seeking to reduce the number of abortions. At times this will require political and legal fights; at times it will require education and the establishment of alternatives to abortion, such as adoption centers." He then warns that progression comes only in small packages, "Unfortunately, such measures are opposed by so-called hard-liners in the pro-life movement. These hard-liners are fools. Because they want to outlaw all abortions, they refuse to settle for stopping some abortions; the consequence is that they end up preventing no abortions."[18]

Yes, we need to restrict abortions through political and legislative means, as D'Souza writes. However, without the support needed to enforce laws, they are meaningless. Therefore, education through grass-roots campaigns is another component that is needed to abort the American holocaust. We have seen diseases cease to exist and ones that are successfully combated through awareness and education. The same must be done with abortion.

We can work to neutralize the pollution of political influence planted in our government institutions of learning by the National Education Association and then seek to educate the public on a voluntary basis.

The options for educating the public on abortions are vast. As mentioned already, you can find a copy of a public videotape showing many of the different medical operations that are done in the United States, but the idea of having a tape of an abortion operation on public record is never really approached. Is it too barbaric? Maybe. I would never wish to view something like that. However, much of the population runs away from the immorality of abortion. Provide them with the ins and outs of the issue, and they are forced to decide.

If you can push something out of your mind long enough, it will eventually go away. The attempt to push the abortion issue out of the view screen is evident in the case where, as of this writing, a woman is suing an abortion clinic because she accidentally saw her murdered child in a jar on the counter. She knew she might have been able to handle it if she didn't have to see or deal with it.[19]

Yet while some women who have had abortions or partial birth abortions have continued throughout their entire lives with emotional anxiety, guilt, and regret through the unwanted memories of renewal on the anniversary date, we must deal with this issue for those who have callused it over, unless you wish to eventually live in a world where the value of human life is at zero.

Without getting in one's face and becoming repulsive, the operation and experience of abortion need to come to life in the minds of Americans. We need to protect and mentor those who have made the deadly mistake of abortion, and we need to make it real for those considering it, without giving negative impressions.

Also, as with showing the barbaric and immoral abortion procedure and aftereffects, we must present a sacred view of life. Through the wondrous technology of ultrasound, we are now able to view breathtaking images of the baby in the womb. If you can really get a grasp on what death is—in this case it is abortion—you also need to get a handle on the awesome power and sanctity of life and the beginning of it. As life is the greatest gift God ever gave to man, we must communicate that.

Still, we also need to pool our resources in political fights, legislative battles, and judicial appointments. But don't hold your breath waiting on Republicans to stand up and fight this battle of principle because they won't do much on a national level.

This is why I mention grassroots campaigns. Although they are not as widespread as a national campaign, they work. The only way the pro-life movement is going to change a substantial number of minds is through local campaigns and battles. Further, I am afraid that a national ban on abortion may do more harm than good at this certain time in society.

On the other hand, this does not necessarily mean that the American view on abortion is completely immoral. Not only has the number of annual abortions decreased over the years, but recent polls show that the American people are coming around. A June 1999 Wirthlin poll found that 62 percent of Americans support legal abortion in very narrow and fewer circumstances. Those circumstances would only be when the pregnancy results from rape or incest or when it threatens the life of the mother.[20]

ALTERNATIVES TO ABORTION

When starting a business, creating a product, or working on just about any project, you seek to create a better market alternative. Whether it is a cheaper product, performs better, or is a new invention, the rule is that you work to create something bigger and better—something people want.

The same is applied to many public policy issues. If you can create a better alternative to divorce, a better alternative to education, a better alternative to your present vehicle, or a better alternative to war, then you will be able to solve the issues. The same goes for abortion, but it is no excuse for the immoral murder that abortion is. The end result is what we all want: reducing the greatest possible number of abortions.

Not to sound too cynical, but in the real world, a society is only moral when it is convenient. With that in mind, here are three workable alternatives:

1. Give financial aid to those considering abortion. A large percentage of those who have abortions are single mothers who do it because of financial reasons or the obvious baggage that comes along with singly raising a child.

2. Make the alternative of adoption an easier system. There is obviously a demand for adopting children in the United States, but the system is so bureaucratic, it's very difficult to work with. Reformation of the system is one of the highest possible goals we can have in winning the war over abortion.

3. Support crisis pregnancy centers. They are on the battle lines and working in the trenches. There are centers across the nation, but there is a need for more. They need support, through financial donations and volunteering.

THE FUTURE

I have exhibited a great love for the Constitution of the United States and the companion document, the Declaration of Independence. Just as Martin Luther King Jr. effectively cited this document as the basis for and justification for the civil rights movement, I believe the same rights to life, liberty, and the pursuit of happiness are inalienable rights of all unborn children, and the systematic slaughter of these helpless human beings must cease.

Unfortunately, it will be a gradual change through shaping our culture, society, and the opinions of the American people—in other words, the goalpost is a long way off. The society I am growing up in says that we should do what we want, when we want it, no matter what. Although I've never been told such a thing, it is expressed through the actions of Americans, such as abortion, the entertainment industry, divorce rates, and the general immorality that is seen.

In the end, the culture of death that is advanced by the moral equivocations and rationalizations that are used to bolster abortion results in more than dead babies. It erodes the foundations of society, morality, and justice. It makes life itself cheap, contingent on convenience. We see the continuation of that logic in the push for euthanasia and assisted suicide. We see it in the increase of crime by younger and younger perpetrators who care nothing for the harm they inflict on their innocent victims. Life means all too little.

I propose to you two futures: the first being a future of morality where generations will be taught the value of life, a future where America will look back on these dark days of abortion and wonder how their parents or grandparents could have allowed such things to happen. Just as we look back with disgust at the days of racism across the nation and the huge membership of groups like the Ku Klux Klan, they will feel the same about abortion.

The second future: imagine the value of life completely debased. Death and destruction are the fruit of this decision, but we are thoroughly desensitized to the issue. Euthanasia would be a daily part of life, abortion would be a necessity, and population control would become as common as taking out the trash.

You can take your pick, but mine will be the pick of morality. A road of hard work, however.

Yes, it will be a long and hard road, but it must be done through changing hearts and lives and putting a moral mark on our culture. Human life may once again be at the greatest value to all Americans.

It will require Americans to unabashedly stand up and hold on to the American principles of morality, life, liberty, and the pursuit of happiness. It's an idea that will be called "intolerant," "politically incorrect," and "radical," but at the end of the day, I know that it is the right thing to do. That kind of ideology has held this nation together through wars, depressions, and overall times of grief. It can hold us together through the war of abortion.

President Ronald Reagan explained this in the greatest possible way: "I hope that when you're my age, you'll be able to say as I have been able to say: We lived in freedom, we lived lives that were a statement, not an apology."[21]

FURTHER READING

Books

- Randy Alcorn, *ProLife Answers to ProChoice Arguments* (Sisters, OR: Multnomah, 2002).

- Theresa Karminski Burke and David C. Reardon, *Forbidden Grief: The Unspoken Pain of Abortion* (Springfield, IL: Acorn Books, 2002).

- David C. Reardon, *Making Abortion Rare* (Springfield, IL: Acorn Books, 1996).

Web Sites

- www.nrlc.org
- www.cwfa.org

Sound Off

★ POLITICS ★

8

Big Daddy

THE NOVEL *1984*, WRITTEN BY GEORGE ORWELL IN 1949, envisions a nightmarish future for the world—a world where everything spoken is heard, every move and every action is recorded and videotaped, and anyone with contempt against the government is disciplined. All are brainwashed to hate the enemy, and all worship "Big Brother."

Orwell's dystopian vision is a glimpse of what theoretically could happen if government is allowed to grow unchecked in its power. While the story takes things to extremes, there is value in exploring an idea to the extreme, as it reveals with startling clarity the end result of a particular idea or philosophy.

The year 1984 came and went a few years before I was born, but Orwell was ahead of his time in conceiving *1984*. With the government continually injecting itself into the private sector and sticking its nose where it doesn't belong, it is apparent that some of the threats presented in Orwell's novel have taken an elementary form. Privacy is disappearing, with more and more surveillance cameras in place, monitoring of phone communication, and monitoring of Internet communication.

Further, because of statist politics, people increasingly are forced to rely and depend on government. From education to farm subsidies, and the September 11, 2001, victim handouts by the government, to the welfare system, relying on government is simply a way of life for some people, which is unfortunate. Welfare, food stamps, Social Security, public education, public housing, and government subsidies—they're all tokens of Orwell's fictional governmental system. Add in the growing encroachment on privacy and civil liberties, and *Hello, Big Brother.*

Some governmental social programs are bigger than others, and some "national security" programs are larger than others, but they all have one thing in common. That is the fact that they are all contributing to bigger government and a greater dependency on government. And the government is glad to do it, that's for sure.

In doing that, the government becomes paternal. George Orwell almost had it right in the fictional reality by naming the government "Big Brother." But our nonfiction version is so paternal government, attempting to "take care" of us, the government would be more appropriately named "Big Daddy." It's less a free republic under the restrictions of the Constitution than the United Socialist States of America.

"Now, Kyle, you're taking it a bit too far. This country hasn't gone off the edge to that extreme."

You may be right, but it cannot be denied that this government is on an unhealthy dose of steroids. It's expanding, growing, and becoming bigger. It's failing now, but a total collapse of government is certain because a complete Big Daddy is not economically feasible, nor morally correct.

POLITICIANS

During election years and right in the heat of the election, the politicians begin to act as if they work for us, the American people. However, somewhere as they go along, they tend to eventually act as if their position is set, and they have some sort of a right to be the president, a congressman, or a governor.

I have to say that not all elected officials are that way; some public officials actually act like public servants and do their duty. Unfortunately, there are too many who believe they are there because they have done something amazingly extraordinary, but in reality citizens decided those people were who they wanted. Nothing too special about that—it's a very simple system.

The trouble comes when the political leaders in our nation have no vision but a quest for power. Issues don't matter, flip-flopping on them is common, and politicalspeak is all that comes from the mouth.

After that, the greed of power manifests itself in issues such as Medicare, Social Security, education, tax cuts, farm subsidies, etc.

FDR'S NEW DEAL OF DESTRUCTION

The growth of government began with deficit financing during the Great Depression. Franklin Delano Roosevelt's "New Deal" created an expansion of our federal government by creating the Federal Emergency Relief Administration, which gave financial relief to the unemployed.

A similar program to boost the government's newly bulging biceps was the Civilian Conservation Corps—a program that put thousands of young men to work on conservation projects, improving national parks and flood control projects. Likewise, the Public Works Administration provided jobs constructing highways, bridges, parks, sewers, schools, and hospitals.

All these programs took vast amounts of money to fund and were actually an early American exercise in Communism Lite. This government was not intended to create and retain programs that employed millions of people. In addition to not being possible, it's not the government's role in society to employ that many people as economic stimulus. But it wasn't to end there. Why whack the constitutional foundation of the nation once when you can do it again? Roosevelt's "Second New Deal" brought in the program we all know and love, Social Security.

It ushered in government funding for unemployment and old age insurance. Financed by taxes on wages, the National Labor Relations Act was established to protect stated rights of unions and to mediate labor-management disputes.

Without a doubt, the hero known as FDR did more harm than good by establishing socialist- and fascist-style government programs, getting involved in the private sector, and managing to pull off the system of Social Security. President Franklin Delano Roosevelt once said, "Like the Bible, it [the Constitution] ought to be read again and again."[1]

If only he had taken his own advice . . .

BIGGER DOESN'T MEAN BETTER (A TIMELINE OF THE U.S. GOVERNMENT)

By the time we land at Harry Truman's administration, the government was still relatively small and America was very strong. In the late forties and early fifties, the government paid for the GI Bill of Rights, one of the largest pieces of legislation at the time. Additionally, since it was right after World War Two, President Truman spent billions on the Marshall Plan to rebuild Europe.

By 1960, the Dwight Eisenhower administration was coming to an end, the nation was in fine shape, the wages of Americans were the highest in the world, and the national debt was closing up, but still recovering from World War Two.

Government was still small, but when President John F. Kennedy took office, he decided to put a stop to that. Government expansion began rapidly, but unfortunately for liberals, his untimely death threatened to slow down the growth. Then Lyndon Johnson took up the reins and carried on his predecessor's big government push.

President Johnson tackled unemployment by proposing a national "War on Poverty." This was a massive government program that called for the creation of new jobs and the building up of economically depressed areas. The two goals were to improve education and to erad-icate poverty, both of which are nearly impossible. Nonetheless, he attempted to obtain his goal by using government programs. The Medicare Act of 1965 was to provide medical care for the elderly through the Social Security system.

The Democrats had the majority in Congress, which gave Johnson almost absolute control of Congress in his effort to pass legislation for the welfare programs and other such unconstitutional desires.

Following Johnson, Republicans, oddly enough, joined the Democrats in their desire for power and big government. President Nixon set the trend in his term of double-digit inflation and high taxes, and deficit spending continued to divert tax dollars to the social and welfare programs.

President Ford was a fiscal conservative, but with a Democratic Congress, spending continued for social programs and the expansion of the Food Stamp Program.

During the Carter administration, minimum wage increased, public service jobs were funded by the federal government for the unem-ployed, Social Security taxes increased, and the federal Department of Education was founded. The national debt rose tremendously, along with the federal deficit.

Increasing federal government borrowing and spending led to inflation, causing the dollar to lose value. The American middle class has paid the price for the forty-year government growth and demand for taxes. The tax code has been a nightmare for some time; citizens of America work until May just to pay their taxes! We give the first five months of our entire earnings to the government to support it. The money drained from the economy to run the massive, untested, unproductive government programs is one of the main ills affecting our economy.

President Reagan wanted the state and local governments to assume more control for government programs, attempting to decrease the power of the national government over the American people. This met with limited success because many people want to depend on the central government to solve their problems.

In the long run and under the Reagan administration, the government became larger, but that can be attributed to the massive defense budget needed during the Cold War. Ronald Reagan took the office of the presidency and made history with the massive tax cut—a whopping 25 percent over three years. After that, the inflation rate dropped dramatically, as did unemployment.

Four years later, the Bill Clinton administration was all but on a campaign to undo the progress and success of the Reagan administration. By hiking taxes, murdering citizens in Texas in the Waco fiasco, bringing the nation into a recession, and ignoring the apparent corporate fraud, his administration is viewed as one of the worst in American history. Vetoing overwhelmingly passed legislation from Congress, he circumvented reform of Medicare and Medicaid, as well as reform in the tax codes.

CONSTITUTIONALITY

For any that have read through the United States Constitution, they know that most of government's post-FDR programs are completely unconstitutional. It's very simple: the Constitution grants government powers, but it hasn't granted power to implement social programs. Nevertheless, even when the Constitution is broken in order to create social programs, the government can't work the programs efficiently. Although many of the government social programs may seem to work in theory, we can see that government programs are falling apart.

Analysts say that by the year 2035, the federal Social Security Fund will hit rock bottom. Therefore, by the time I retire, I won't be receiving those funds, but I will start investing early in an effort to live independently in later life—which should have been the standard in the first place.

We don't have to wait thirty-plus years to see the demise of the public education system. It's floundering even now.

In addition, not much convincing is needed to see that the welfare system is in shambles. The welfare system doesn't work because there is no incentive for recipients to get jobs. If I find homeless people on the street, instead of giving them money, I would help them find a job—if they actually want one. The result of handing out money will keep them in the same pathetic situation. Far from just smoothing over societal inequities, welfare actually encourages resentment in society. Thomas Jefferson warned that a wise and good government "shall not take from the mouth of labor the bread it has earned."

You could write entire books going over the failures of the state. Many have. The bloated organization that we call the "government" is a monster, unable to efficiently function. If government worked and could work properly, many would have no problem with the huge size of the government. However, it is impossible for the government, being as big as it is, to function efficiently.

EXPANDING GOVERNMENT: LESS PRIVACY

Since the September 11, 2001, terrorist attacks in New York and Washington, D.C., the government has increased its powers concerning privacy, searches, and seizures. President Bush and his White House buddies passed the USA Patriot Act after the attacks—it's one of the most freedom-thieving bills in U.S. history and radically stands in opposition to the conservative principle of smaller government.

Fear is an extremely powerful tool and, when used properly, it can be useful. In July 2002, President Bush unveiled a new homeland security strategy for the nation. The ninety-page report calls for drastic changes in state and federal law, changes in military management, and it outlines many other desired programs and initiatives. The White House practically authored it, demanding certain components and financial plans. Although security is a must in the post-9/11 world, the proposed Department of Homeland Security plan was nothing but an enormous increase in government and bureaucracy.[2]

There are several disturbing initiatives planned in Bush's national strategy, such as deployment of military troops in domestic situations, federal insurance for terrorist attacks, and other such unconstitutional initiatives. However, in this terrorism age, the Constitution need not apply.

This is a further example of adding onto government to fix government problems. Logic does not appear to be on that side.

While the plan for the department appeared to be the way to go, the simple fact is that such a crucial and huge office will always become bogged down and turn into one of the nation's largest bureaucracies—the essence of what such a department is supposed to fix. When you put such tremendous responsibility and workload on any bureaucratically managed workforce, the end result will be a bigger, slower, and inefficient agency.

However, taking a look at the current system, one could see that if we just run the system the way it was intended, our government would work properly. Having a bureaucracy running another bureaucracy will accomplish nothing. Look at the INS, IRS, FEMA, and dozens of other agencies.

A growing trend since the presidency of Franklin Delano Roosevelt has been that the simple solution to all problems is the creation and growth of new legislation and more government. Just as the House and Senate continually pass more and more gun control legislation (as if illegally possessing and illegally firing an illegally acquired gun and then illegally killing a person weren't already, er, *illegal*), the government continually grows to fix problems. Instead, government should enforce the original gun legislation and reform the system to make departments and agencies work. A question that we must ask is, Are we certain we want to make our government bigger?

Anytime government is bigger, freedom becomes smaller. Certainly, the chance of encroachment on liberties and freedom is a real threat that comes along with homeland "security"—this has been communicated through the USA Patriot Act and other such legislation.

SUBSIDIES: REDISTRIBUTING WEALTH

Under the name of "economic growth," the government has taken it upon itself to take our money and give it to businesses. A great example would be what happened in Oklahoma City, Oklahoma, in 2001.

Oklahoma City wanted to lend $18 million to Bass Pro Shop to build a Sportsman's Center. The plan was that in fifteen years, the store would pay off the loan and would increase economic growth. However, a stir was raised and many got upset. An independent study showed that it wouldn't pay itself off, would benefit a handful of business owners, would create an antibusiness environment, and many found it offensive. The essence of the deal was that the government would take money from citizens in order to help someone else.[3]

The federal and state governments do things to that tune very often. By interfering with the private sector, the government is turning America into a socialist and fascist nation. It's the same concept as that of a man, by way of force, taking $1,000 from each family in his neighborhood in order to help his friend start a business. In return, the business may help a handful of those in the neighborhood, and the business owner might pay off the "loan."

On the national level, President Bush pushed for, agreed with, and signed the farm legislation in the summer of 2002. The bill, which is thrown into the stack alongside other unconstitutional legislation, takes money from one person's hand and gives it to someone else—a legalized theft operation that the Constitution does not allow. Again, this bill, as is true for so many others, goes against the conservative principle of smaller government.

In addition, you have the September 11 charity program, in which the government gave millions of dollars to those victimized by the terrorist attacks. The Oklahoma City bombing victims and their families could be next to receive millions from the government. While this may sound fine, it goes back to the concerns of Davy Crockett that a precedent such as this will open the spigot of the federal budget and allow for any victim to receive some sort of severance pay. Such an ability is economically unfeasible.

What is one of the single greatest problems facing our nation today, and what is the solution? Societal dependence on government. That dependence is leading to an all-out "Big Daddy" paternalistic government, as if we're a nation of kids that can't grow up and take care of ourselves. A main reason we are heading toward such a failure in society and government is the selfishness of many and, ultimately, the irresponsibility of too many. Anyone can watch or read the news for a short amount of time and see selfishness, greed, and irresponsibility in not only legislators and public officials, but in ordinary American citizens.

For a long time the reason for the growth of government has been handouts—not just the millions given to World Trade victims. There is much more than that. Recently, citizens have been demanding a prescription drug plan. Still, for some time now, more and more welfare has been demanded, as well as Medicare, Social Security, corporate subsidies, and a long list of other government programs including wasteful pork-barrel programs shipped back to congressional districts with a high-priced regularity.

"What's wrong with all these things?" some may ask. Answer: they are taking our country toward a cliff of destruction. The government can only handle so much. It is impossible to give away services and money and cut taxes. Therefore, the threat of a continually rising national debt remains a reality—eventually leading to a crash-and-burn situation in the nation.

The people of the United States today are the undeserving heirs of such patriots as Benjamin Franklin, Thomas Jefferson, James Madison, John Adams, and many more Founding Fathers. The Founders sacrificed so much for their posterity and left such a legacy, but most today are entirely undeserving of it.

Two words America must hear: *grow up!* This is especially important for people my age who are now forming their political ideas in conjunction with progression to adulthood.

In contrast to what is in abundance in our nation today, responsibility in America was and is a requirement. Without it, the Constitution is just a piece of paper, the Declaration of Independence is of no importance, and the eventual destruction of limited government and freedom is certain.

SUCCESS WITHOUT A GOVERNMENT GRANT

With the free market, small business owners and entrepreneurs are the backbone of the United States economy. Instead of letting government become larger and infect the private sector, look at the successes of others without the help of the government:

- Radio king Rush Limbaugh reaches an estimated 22 million listeners each day through over 600 radio stations. As he has stated on his radio show many times, just a shade under a decade ago he was far from his current economic status, his political position and respect, and his influence on the everyday American.

- Although his parents wanted him to be a doctor, he went against their wishes, and Michael Dell built his first few computers while attending the University of Texas. His company, Dell Computers, is now one of the largest computer manufacturers in the country.

- When Sam Walton, from Kingfisher, Oklahoma, had just come out of college, he started a career in the retail business. In 1962, he opened his first Wal-Mart store, and a chain of stores sprang up across America. Before he died, his franchise became the largest retailer in the United States.

- Even WorldNetDaily and WND Books show the opportunity of the free market. Joseph and Elizabeth Farah started a small news Web site in 1997—little did they realize that five years later they would be announcing a joint venture with publishing giant Thomas Nelson.

Times are tough, the economy is down, and the unemployment rate is at the highest in eight years, but the market is coming back. Learn from the examples above. Everyone has a chance. Entrepreneurship is what drives the economy of America. With that opportunity, everyone has the chance to find work or create work by starting a small business.

But many Americans believe that government is the answer, and government should play a part in providing housing, money, and support. In contrast, I sincerely believe big government is *not* the answer. No offense to the government road workers, but when riding down the road, you see one man working and ten men watching. This is essentially the way most areas of government work. It is between hard and impossible to fire a government worker based on performance. I don't know about you, but I don't want to rely on that sort of government.

If you ask a big-government liberal what makes America great, he or she will most likely reply that it is freedom. Yet with more government comes less freedom—totally contradicting that point of view.

The less government there is, the better off freedom is. As the Constitution tells us, the U.S. government is supposed to "establish justice, insure domestic tranquility, provide for the common defense, promote the general welfare, and secure the blessings of liberty to ourselves and our posterity." When it goes beyond this charge, it not only flounders at its new tasks but tends to fail at its constitutionally mandated duties as well.

Former President Ronald Reagan stressed during his presidency that the free market knows best and should decide, rather than the government. The market economy will always rule over the command economy.

LIBERALISM: A FORCE BEHIND BIG DADDY

With the founding of the United States came unprecedented freedom and the greatest country on the planet, so why would anyone choose to denigrate freedom? The answer is found in the essence of liberalism and socialism—bigger government, more aid and social programs.

The Founders of our country were very careful in the Constitution to bar democracy from invading our nation, but the Constitution is nothing but a piece of paper to many elected officials. Moreover, many have taken our country to be a democracy without a real thought—including the president. Benjamin Franklin didn't call our nation a "republic" for nothing.

A democratic nation cannot stand; it will always fall because the minute the population sees that it can receive aid, money, social programs—government handouts—it will elect new officials to meet its greed, and government will always hand it out.

"What's this have to do with liberalism?" you might ask. Liberalism has everything to do with greed and that alone. Thus, liberals exploit American government's democratic features and buy votes and power with aid, money, benefits, etc. It comes down to one thing: when the road of principles meets the road of greed, greed is almost always chosen.

One example is the greed of government subsidies in private industry. Many take advantage of the government's willingness to get involved in the private sector, but in doing so, they compromise the future of capitalism—the mixing of private and public is fascist to the core.

And liberalism and socialism have made their way into government through social programs such as Social Security, Medicare, welfare, and other such government programs. While the people are supposed to invest their money wisely and make their own decisions to have a healthy retirement, government has stepped in and attempted to take care of the nation.

In terms of welfare, many of those on the welfare payroll are physically and mentally capable of going out and obtaining employment, but laziness has replaced free-market incentive. Furthermore, besides extreme greed replacing principles and responsibility, ignorance and short-term thought replace rational decisions and ideals.

When socialism and liberalism infect government, no question is brought up about whether the government has the right or resources to carry out a socialist program. As a result, some might get the good end of the deal and receive what they want, but in the long run, government is made bigger and taxes are raised, resulting in a worse life for everyone.

While the average liberal is different from the high-profile liberal politician, the concepts are basically the same: bigger government through handouts, social programs, aid, and other forms of welfare. Still, politicians hide behind doublespeak and carry out their agendas under the guise of statements such as, "It's for the children," and "It's about women's choice," while carrying out programs in the name of "minorities."

Liberalism is a mixture of all-out greed, irresponsibility, ignorance, and irrational programs and decisions. Those warped foundations have made their way to government and created a government that is a monster. That monster has all but replaced the role the American people should fill with charity, kindness, hard work, and sacrifice.

REWRITING HISTORY

The danger of having a federal education system is not only terrible results, but also brainwashing those who don't know much better. Evidence shows that the government has been rewriting history through federal and state curricula.

Clearly, history has been rewritten in the public curricula of America. President Abraham Lincoln is looked at as the most truthful president in our history, and Franklin Delano Roosevelt is portrayed as the greatest president—the one who took us out of the Great Depression and won World War Two.

Critical information about our domestic history somehow always seems to evade the textbooks. In a textbook, for instance, you wouldn't find FDR illegally reseating an entire Supreme Court because they ruled his programs unconstitutional. In schools, all you hear about is the sinless Union of the Civil War, skipping out on the atrocities committed, while the Confederacy is painted as an evil, evil body. Both sides were wrong in decisions and actions they made, but the government, knowing best, rewrites history through government schools.

Thomas Jefferson, the father of the Declaration of Independence, is not portrayed as a fierce patriot, going through all the great things he did. On the contrary, he is portrayed as the man who "invented" separation of church and state and was an owner of slaves—Jefferson's own humanity and internal struggles about slavery are glossed over, and students are served up a caricature of one of America's greatest patriots instead.

AN AMERICAN EXPERIMENT

"The sacred fire of liberty and the destiny of the republican model of government are justly considered," President George Washington said in his First Inaugural Address, "as deeply, perhaps finally, staked on the experiment entrusted to the hands of the American people." The responsibility of that experiment includes the requirement of the people to keep and protect the inalienable rights that were given by God and granted by the Constitution.

Benjamin Franklin warned the American people not to trade liberty for security and said those who would give up liberty for security deserve neither. Yet just like every other piece of advice the Founders gave us, Americans have taken it with a grain of salt and have forgotten about it.

This is evident in one of the scariest polls ever released. In August 2002, a very disturbing annual "State of the First Amendment" poll was released by the First Amendment Center. The results of the poll showed a dramatically high dependence on and trust in government, but also showed extremely high ignorance regarding the purpose and the content of the Constitution. The poll, which was conducted by the University of Columbia's Center for Survey Research and Analysis, found that 49 percent of Americans believe that the First Amendment goes too far in the rights it grants and guarantees.[4]

The statistics also show that half of Americans say the press has been too aggressive in asking government officials for information regarding the war on terrorism. However, the American public is once again in disagreement with the Founders, for Thomas Jefferson said, "The only security of all is in a free press. The force of public opinion cannot be resisted when permitted freely to be expressed."[5]

According to this poll, more than 40 percent of Americans also said that academic freedom should be limited so that professors cannot criticize government military policy.

Yet it goes on to even more disturbing statistics. About half of those surveyed said the FBI should be able to monitor religious groups in the name of national security, even if that means infringing on religious freedoms. These answers are being provided by people who couldn't even say the First Amendment grants freedom of speech. Moreover, only 2 percent of those surveyed could recite every right the amendment grants!

In times of war, reason is replaced with fear, and government capitalizes on that. With the USA Patriot Act, the government edged into the rights of the people, giving great power to the attorney general.

But the First Amendment grants freedom of speech, freedom of the press, freedom of religion, as well as the right to peaceably assemble and petition the government. These things are not privileges granted by government, but legal rights given by God that we can exercise even if we offend someone or agitate some government official. If left unprotected, the rights of the people will continue to be usurped by politicians—and those "representatives" know they can get away with more and more. The only things that make America unique are these constitutional rights that have been granted and given by God. But Americans are asking our government to take these rights away for security! Much has changed since the founding of our country.

Americans are still badly out of touch with reality, and the road we are headed down is lunacy. Level heads and responsible minds are in the minority these days. Government has become blindly supported . . . and that's called patriotism?

GOVERNMENT FAILURES

It's bad enough that the government has gotten involved in the private sector by way of welfare, Social Security, unemployment checks, etc. However, what makes it worse is that when the government becomes involved through these programs, they all fail!

The basic rule you learn in economics is that "there ain't no such thing as a free lunch." No object is free. You may be getting free government health care, but someone paid for it. You may be getting welfare, but someone paid for it. You may be getting 9/11 payout funds, but someone paid for it.

Theoretically, these programs would work, but it would require more money going in than out. A balanced budget would become government's impossible-to-find Holy Grail. A Democratic-Republican form of government cannot exist as partly socialist and expect to, in the long term, exist. You can only tax people so far, so long. Since all these government transfers fail to actually make money—they merely move it from here to there—over time they slow down the economy to the point of immobility.

CONCLUSION

Through the paternal state of the government, citizens rely on government. It's human nature to take an easy route and throw out the work ethic.

Almost the whole nation is educated through public schools. It is no surprise that in those public schools, social issues and education take a high priority, in some cases, over traditional and basic subjects. The teaching needed to educate young people in their future business career is not supplied but thoroughly ignored. Therefore, because upcoming generations are not schooled in business and economics, many are incapable of being successful entrepreneurs without attending those classes in higher education.

Basing their actions on lazy human nature, many choose to rely on government. Capitalizing on that, Big Daddy will happily supply the needs, creating a dependent nation. But if the government is Daddy and we're the children, there is definitely some child abuse going on.

If you have small children, you are going to keep all potentially dangerous or deadly substances or objects out of reach of the children. Additionally, you want to be a shoulder of support for your children and help them with what they need. What the government is doing is almost the same thing—except the nation isn't composed of children. Because of this, Big Daddy's motivation is not so much love and caring as it is the desire to feel superior and important and to control. Big Daddy is taking our guns away and working hard to outlaw cigarettes— because it doesn't trust children, *but adults* with these items. This is all done not out of concern for our well-being but to dominate and create a submissive nation. At first glance, government may appear to be a tool to help us, but that's definitely not so. It's more like a somewhat-comfortable prison cell.

How can I be so sure of this? It's because we have seen many of these programs in other countries; they have not worked and have even made matters worse. But government officials continue to push for these programs.

Remember as concerns the U.S., this is the same government that has a $6 trillion debt and a growing list of agencies that create the largest bureaucracy on the planet. Do you really want to depend on that? I hope not.

The famous words uttered by President Abraham Lincoln—"That government of the people, by the people, for the people, shall not perish from the earth"—do not seem to be fully true today. However, what is true is that the government is still of the people. America, *wake up!* Now that our elected officials have taken it upon themselves to disregard everything the Constitution says, we must recognize what is happening and not stand for it!

Ronald Reagan, a visionary leader, a man who knew what conservatism was, and one of our greatest presidents, had it right on government when he said, "There seems to be an increasing awareness of something we Americans have known for some time: That the ten most dangerous words in the English language are, 'Hi, I'm from the Government and, I'm here to help.'"[6]

FURTHER READING

Books

- Frederic Bastiat, *The Law* (Irvington-on-Hudson: Foundation for Economic Education, 1998).

- James Bovard, *Freedom in Chains* (New York: St. Martin's Griffin, 1999).

- David Limbaugh, *Absolute Power* (Washington, DC: Regnery, 2001).

- George Orwell, *1984* (New York: Signet Classic, 1984). Many printings available.

- Jonathan Rauch, *Government's End* (New York: Public Affairs, 1999).

- Ronald Reagan, *Reagan: In His Own Hand,* edited by Kiron K. Skinner et al. (New York: Free Press, 2001).

- Walter Williams, *More Liberty Means Less Government* (Stanford: Hoover, 1999).

Web Sites

- www.cato.org
- www.fee.org
- www.heritage.org

9

Dividing the Line

"Separation of church and state."

What do you think of when hearing that phrase? Some have anger. Some think of the American Civil Liberties Union. Some have positive reactions. Some think of it as a political myth. And still others think of it as a battle cry.

As I became aware of current events and politics, it was quite confusing to figure out what's real and what's an illusion. I started out believing guns were extremely dangerous, racism against blacks was still rampant, and separation between religious beliefs and government was your average, constitutional requirement. However, if you read any part of this book, you know that I have changed a little bit.

The separation of church and state issue is one of the most confused ideas of politics and government. I got suckered into thinking it was law, millions still are suckered, and it goes much deeper than the surface—definitely not a shallow issue.

Thus, opinions on both sides are strong. You may believe, as liberals do, that it's the law and it's just. You may be a moderate, not really sure what side to take. Or you may be a traditional conservative, believing politics and religion go hand in hand.

Whatever the case may be, it has become one of the highly political and passionate issues of American politics in recent years. The key players: the American Center for Law and Justice, Wall Builders, the American Civil Liberties Union, the American Conservative Union, and Americans United for the Separation of Church and State. All having a large amount of political power, it has turned into a highly contested and debated topic of late. But no matter how hotly debated and contested it has become, the majority of Americans have grown to accept the liberal view as reality.

Initial perception is reality for many Americans on this issue. The perception of a sharp divide between church and state is implanted in the government schools, as it is taught as law. Unfortunately, these public institutions of learning are teaching revisionist history.

The conservatives always tend to lose because they are not organized. The American Left, however, is highly organized. Leftist organizations support each other, they share resources, they work together, and they help each other obtain their warped agendas. It's no surprise then that the separation of church and state organizations are pretty good friends with the National Education Association—which shapes the teaching of America's schools, thus shaping public opinion and sympathy toward the separation viewpoint.

THE ISSUE

The basic idea behind the separation of church and state: the United States government should have nothing to do with religion at all, and religion should have nothing to do with government at all.

Based on falsehood, belief in the separation doctrine has been used for political reasons more than a striving for truth in the issue. Under the banner of "constitutional rights," the American Civil Liberties Union has worked at completely making government unchristian.

The idea behind a separation between religion, especially Christianity (ever notice how the First Amendment is often used to defend other religions but to attack Christianity?), and state is supposedly a campaign to make government unbiased. Yet governments are instituted by men, run by men, and completely controlled by men. The truth is that men are fallible, finite, and cannot remain sinless. Mistakes will be made, men will be biased, and they will have their opinions, whether they be for the good or the bad.

But instead of merely rooting out bias (as impossible as that is), it has often been used by antireligionists as a means to silence religious expression, almost like the propaganda tools examined in Chapter 2: "Intolerance to the Extreme." So bias isn't removed; instead, one bias trumps the other with the help of the state. The separation doctrine is used by the Left as a silencer for prayer in schools, prayer in government, Bible studies, and for diffusing any form of Christianity in a government workplace.

Most people assume that the separation of church and state comes from the First Amendment. It doesn't, but because Americans are extremely uneducated about the Constitution, this gives great credence to the Left's separation of church and state argument.

The First Amendment of the United States Constitution states, "Congress shall make no law respecting an establishment of religion, or prohibiting the free exercise thereof . . ." The words *separation, church*, and *state* do not appear once, as you can see. But who needs facts to have an argument these days?

The confusion is in a distortion of words. *Congress* is substituted with *government, shall make no law* is substituted with *shall not be, respecting* is substituted with *involved, an establishment of religion* is substituted with *with any form of* any *religion or morality*, and *or prohibiting the free exercise thereof* is removed entirely.

Thus, the dream of the ACLU is that the first part of the First Amendment states, "Government shall not be involved with any form of religion or morality." From the stripping of the Ten Commandments from most all public buildings, to the abolition of prayer in schools, to the opposition of vouchers, it's all about taking religion out of public discourse and programs.

Besides hijacking the Constitution, these anti-American leftists have won the award for the most-out-of-context quote. The phrase "separation of church and state" was "coined" by Thomas Jefferson when explaining the newly created Constitution. Thomas Jefferson's letter to Danbury Baptist Association of Danbury, Connecticut, was written to calm their fears about Congress choosing any single Christian denomination in order to make the "state" denomination, as was the case with the Anglican Church in England and Virginia.

In the letter to the Baptists, who had experienced severe persecution for their faith, Jefferson wrote,

> Believing with you that religion is a matter which lies solely between Man & his God, that he owes account to none other for his faith or his worship, that the legitimate powers of government reach actions only, & not opinions, I contemplate with sovereign reverence that act of the whole American people which declared that their legislature should "make no law respecting an establishment of religion, or prohibiting the free exercise thereof," thus building a wall of separation between Church & State.

First, Thomas Jefferson is treated with more respect than almost all the Founders, his writings and opinions were and still are some of the greatest documents that give us insight into the revolutionary thinking of that day, and he almost single-handedly wrote the document that declared the freedom and principles of this nation. However, knowing that, we can't take this letter as the authority on the First Amendment because Jefferson wasn't even a delegate at the Constitutional Convention.

Although he cannot be taken as the authority on the First Amendment, his point is valid if taken in context. "Religious liberty and separation of church and state are the cornerstones of the American way of life," maintains Americans United for the Separation of Church and State. "The Framers of the Constitution designed the First Amendment's religion clauses to embrace two key concepts: the government will not endorse or oppose any particular religious viewpoint (or religion generally), and will not interfere with the right of citizens to practice their faith. As Thomas Jefferson put it, the American people created a 'wall of separation between church and state.'"[1]

It's all in the context.

David Barton, known as one of the greatest American historians on colonial times, explained this in the December 2001 issue of WorldNetDaily's *Whistleblower:* "Jefferson understood [the Baptists'] concern. In his response he assured them that the free exercise of religion was indeed an unalienable right and would not be meddled with by the government. Jefferson pointed out to them that there was a 'wall of separation of between church and state' to ensure that the government would never interfere with religious activities."[2]

Based on the statements made by Jefferson, the other Founders, and the original state constitutions, we can see that religion was and is intended to play a major role in government; many colonial leaders and statesmen were Christian ministers. Their idea was obviously not to fully separate church and state—otherwise the entire age of the American Revolution was a total contradiction. Why would they make such laws, then turn around to pray, levy money for printing Bibles, and write state constitutions that, in some cases, required a profession of faith in God and Christianity to hold public office? These people weren't dumb, and they obviously wouldn't start this nation out the gate with such an idiotic step contrary to their beliefs.

The principle of separation of church and state can be easily explained. When one has an outdoor aviary with liberty birds, such as pigeons, there is a special chute that allows the birds to enter, but not come out. In the evening, the bird keeper puts a mesh cone in the entry hole, so they can go into the aviary, but are unable to exit through the small end.

This is the way separation of church and state is. Religion can enter into government, in the form of prayers, political figures, programs, etc. However, government cannot exit into the religious playing field. Religion can intervene with government, but government cannot intervene with religion. The First Amendment prohibits congressional respect of religion but also protects the freedom of religion. This freedom also extends into the public arena.

The errors involved in the separation of church and state argument extend to the powers of government. The separation of church and state crowd has said that it is unconstitutional for prayer meetings and Bible studies to take place on government property—specifically, public schools. However, the only group of people who can actually violate the Constitution are those who are under the color of law. Because the Constitution applies only to government and its restrictions and powers, it doesn't have anything to do with individual citizens having Bible studies.

The Constitution restricts government. It does not specify what an American can or cannot do; it specifies what the government can and cannot do.

The argument against church and state separation cannot stand alone with a study of the Constitution; beyond that, the original intent of the Founders is also relevant. To back up and show the evidence of such things, we must examine what the Founders wrote, said, believed, and we must read the laws they created for the newly founded country.

ORIGINAL INTENT

There is a lot of contention in the debate over the question of what the Founders originally intended for the nation. Yet finding the original intent of the founders of this nation is not difficult—the words and ideas of the Founders are as close as an Internet connection or library. In addition to looking at the writings of the Constitutional Convention delegates, studying the original, pre–Civil War, state constitutions is vital.

The Supremacy Clause, implemented after the Civil War, all but destroyed the rights of the states to make such decisions. It circumvented the will of the people and is responsible for the national debates run by special-interest groups and political machines. But that certainly wasn't the aim of the Founders. By looking at the original state constitutions, we can see the framers' handle on the issues and see the way our nation was intended to be run in relation to the government and religions.

The 1817 state constitution of Mississippi says, "No person who denies the being of God or a future state of rewards and punishments shall hold any office in the civil department of the State."[3] They didn't seem to be a bit biased, did they? As an example of the culture at the time, the government was obviously merged with religion—in Mississippi at least.

Still, it doesn't even begin to stop there—or even slow down.

The 1778 state constitution of South Carolina states, "That all persons and religious societies who acknowledge that there is one God, and a future state of rewards and punishments, and that God is publicly to be worshipped, shall be freely tolerated . . . That all denominations of Christian[s] . . . in this State, demeaning themselves peaceably and faithfully, shall enjoy equal religious and civil privileges."[4]

The 1777 Georgia state constitution starts out, "We, the people of Georgia, relying upon protection and guidance of Almighty God, do ordain and establish this Constitution."[5]

These people that established the states and communities that began the nation we now call the "United States" obviously intended deep religious influence on the workings of government. They put words honoring God and submitting to God in the founding documents that created the nation.

Yet Americans United for the Separation of Church and State still says, "The Constitution mandates it. Most Americans believe in it."[6] However puzzling, the evidence of religion in government marches on.

The 1780 Massachusetts constitution reads as follows: "We, therefore, the people of Massachusetts, acknowledging, with grateful hearts, the goodness of the great Legislator of the universe, in affording us, in the course of His providence [an opportunity to form a compact]: . . . and devoutly imploring His direction in so interesting a design, . . . [establish this Constitution]."[7]

The constitution of the state of Delaware originally stated in section XXII:

Every person who shall be chosen a member of either house, or appointed to any office or place of trust . . . shall . . . make and subscribe the following declaration, to wit: "I, _____, do profess faith in God the Father, and in Jesus Christ His only Son, and in the Holy Ghost, one God, bless for evermore; I do acknowledge the Holy Scriptures of the Old and New Testament to be given by divine inspiration."[8]

Up until 1818, the state of Connecticut's constitution contained the wording:

The People of this State . . . by the Providence of God . . . hath the sole and exclusive right of governing themselves as a free, sovereign, and independent State . . . and forasmuch as the free fruition of such liberties and privileges as humanity, civility, and Christianity call for, as is due to every man in his place and proportion . . . hath ever been, and will be the tranquility and stability of Churches and Commonwealth; and the denial thereof, the disturbances, if not the ruin of both.[9]

The evidence only mounts, as document after document reveals the original intent of the Founders. That intent was obviously not meant to require a separation of church and state as the Supreme Court ruled in 1947.[10]

"The Christian religion must be the basis of any government intended to secure the rights and privileges of a free people." This doesn't sound a wee bit politically incorrect, does it? Probably a radical statement by today's standards, but not by the standards of Noah Webster as he wrote in his *American Dictionary of the English Language* in 1828.[11]

The original intent of the Founders is more than obvious. Their views have been obvious not only in relation to the church and government, but also their deep-seated beliefs in the Bible.

Fisher Ames said, "Should not the Bible regain the place it once held as a schoolbook? Its morals are pure, its examples are captivating and noble . . . In no Book is there so good English, so pure and so elegant, and by teaching all the same they will speak alike, and the Bible will justly remain the standard of language as well as of faith."[12]

These deep religious ideas were not isolated. They were the belief at the time as they created the base for the American nation. If the ACLU and Americans United for the Separation of Church and State can ramble on and on about the original intent of the Founders about religion and government, they cannot responsibly ignore these facts.

The facts are these: the Founders wanted a government that was run by moral and religious people. John Adams said, "Our Constitution was made only for a moral and religious people. It is wholly inadequate to the government of any other."[13] Maybe a little too radical for Nadine Strossen, president of the ACLU, but it works for me.

Next, in order to keep the government's actions just, they needed religion. There is no basis for justice without morality, and there is no basis for morality without religion. That is not to say that an atheist is without morals, but what is the reasoning behind morality without a belief in something greater? Without a bar of justice beyond mere men in the here and now, who's to say what's really right and wrong? The buck stops with either God or nobody.

Last, you would think these atheists would show a little respect. Without Christianity, or at least the Judeo-Christian values, they probably wouldn't enjoy freedom to attack the source of their liberty.

The main reason for fleeing from the tyranny of Great Britain was the freedom of religion. A freedom that would allow anyone to practice their spiritual beliefs anytime, anywhere, in nearly any way they wished. As far as the Founders were concerned, faith and freedom went hand in hand. Said John Adams, "[The] general principles on which the fathers achieved independence were . . . the general principles of Christianity . . . I will avow that I then believed, and now believe, that those great principles of Christianity are as eternal and immutable as the existence and attributes of God."[14] But, alas, those principles are now under attack again by the powers of special-interest efforts and lobbying in Washington.

Thomas Jefferson's thoughts were far ahead of their time when he said, "God who gave us life gave us liberty. And can the liberties of a nation be thought secure when we have removed their only firm basis, a conviction in the minds of the people that these liberties are a gift of God? That they are not to be violated but with His wrath? Indeed, I tremble for my country when I reflect that God is just; that His justice cannot sleep forever."[15]

DIVIDING THE COMMUNITY

When a line is divided between church and state, it also marks a line in the sand between communities when their traditions and actions are threatened. So is the case when the American Civil Liberties Union dispatches its army of lawyers to small, rural towns because they had the audacity to pray in schools or public places, or dare to put a "God Bless America" note on a public marquee. Scary thought, isn't it?

That was the case in Franklinton, Louisiana, when local residents paid road crews to erect signs on the highway that read, "Jesus is Lord over Franklinton." Yes, this is a violation of the separation of church and state! Why? Because, argued the ACLU, they were put on state roads. Maybe we could consider banning all forms of religion from state and interstate highways. The ACLU filed a federal lawsuit against the town seeking to remove the signs, resulting in a large fiasco. No one had complained about the signs since they had been put up. A card-carrying ACLU member, no doubt, was passing through Franklinton and realized that such a major "problem" must be dealt with, pronto.

Why would it bother the ACLU that signs were put on state roads that announced the religious conviction of Franklinton? The agenda goes beyond me, but it has increasingly become clear that the agenda isn't in tune with American values.

As with the demoralizing of Louisiana state roads, such has been done with schools. Most recently, I remember when the courts ruled that a prayer couldn't be led over the loudspeakers at high school football games. It caused a stir in many communities. Yet in our local community, we went ahead to pray without any direction from the announcer, and it was the same wherever the games were played around the state.

This shows the determination of Americans and shows that we are not willing to have and do not favor such division. If it were the case, would you believe those football game attendants would have recited an undirected prayer, would there still be Bible studies in high schools across the country, and would presidents still have National Days of Prayer? I doubt it.

Another case that is much like the prohibition of school prayer is the Ninth District Court of Appeals decision that a school-led reciting of the Pledge of Allegiance is unconstitutional. You guessed it. Separation of church and state is the culprit once again. According to the decision, the words *under God* make the Pledge illegal. The Founders must be rolling in their graves.

This Pledge case is an able example of what happens when big-city, limousine liberalism attacks America. They want to remove these traditions, values, and religion from the everyday life that is known as American culture. Hearing stories like this, I have been convinced that the campaign to divide the line is insincere, without regard to the original intent of the Founders and the laws communicated in the Constitution, and is more a campaign to demoralize the nation by taking all things religious out of anything public other than an allegiance to the First Amendment. If we cannot continue to exercise our freedom of religion, then we will have lost the very element that created the greatest country that ever existed.

As I was getting caught up with the news one cold evening, I noticed the headline "ACLU goes to bat for Satan." Yes, the ACLU stuck its nose where it didn't belong once again. In January 2002, the union threatened a lawsuit against the mayor of Inglis, Florida—a town with the small population of 1,400. Her crime? She had the nerve to officially proclaim the banishment of Satan within the city limits from the posts at the town's entry points. Mayor Carolyn Risher insisted that she didn't wish to offend anyone but was simply praying for the community. It would be interesting to see how Satan and the American Civil Liberties Union formulated their case.[16]

There was yet again another upset for the organization Americans United for the Separation of Church and State when the House of Representatives and the United States Senate passed legislation allowing the use of the Capitol Rotunda for prayer sessions. "If members of Congress want a religious service, they can go to their houses of worship. The U.S. Capitol is not a revival tent," they whined.[17]

Contrary to what they say, I find it very ironic that the beliefs, virtues, and ideals of the American Revolution are being attacked on a daily basis under the banner of the "Constitution" and "freedom." When the First Congress convened, the leaders of America were afraid that their experiment would fail and the government would fall, but they prayed to God for His blessing and guidance. Maybe if they hadn't, the result would have been different.

SEPARATION OF CHURCH AND STATE— FOR REAL

What is separation of church and state? In bottom line, cold, hard reality, what is the division, and what's the purpose? As conceived by modern-day liberals, it's totally bogus and completely nonfactual.

So, what's the reasoning behind it? Well, as with many political ideas, the leaders know what's really going on behind the scenes. They usually have some sort of scheme. With Jesse Jackson, he has a thirst for power, and he's taking advantage of the black community. With Democrats, they scare seniors for power. And it goes on and on, so it would be redundant to list them all. But the basic principle is that there is always some sort of agenda behind things.

Franklin Delano Roosevelt was perhaps the greatest liberal politician America has ever seen. That is not to say he was a good president, his policies were just, or his ideas and actions were right. Yet he was an absolute master at what he did. One of the brilliant things he said that is still true today is that everything in politics happens for a reason. There are few accidents. It's almost like a chess game or a Broadway show.

Thus, campaigns like the separation of church and state, abortion campaigns, and the so-called quest for educating America on the part of the NEA all tend to have ulterior motives other than what are shown. This case of the "unconstitutional" Pledge of Allegiance further exposes the fact that such decisions are not made by strict interpretation of law and the Constitution, but opinions seeping into their rulings by antireligious atheists.

The agenda of these highly funded, liberal organizations is, many times, that of the ideals of secular humanism. This is obviously the case with separation of church and state. Why else would the campaign ignore the apparent religious roots our nation was founded on, throw away the original intent, and demoralize the public sector of the United States? The evidence has been presented, the answers are here, but they are ignored.

There is definitely an agenda out there to attack the ideals of America. It's highly funded, very supported in high political circles, and has an endless stream of donations each year.

CONCLUSION

We have this problem, so what are we to do about it? First thing is that the evidence is on the side of the antiseparation viewpoint. Second, you can see when the idea of separation goes awry, as lawsuits attack small and isolated towns in the heartland of America.

The separation of church and state really doesn't benefit anyone but the minority political view. Unfortunately, this nation has become a place where the minority rules the majority.

Getting past that, is there a solution to this problem? One thing I know for sure is that no legislation, court ruling, or political campaign is going to make much difference in this debate.

The solutions to many of our problems in America are truly just to keep on keeping on with daily life. Although political problems cannot begin to be compared with terrorism, the people of Israel and now America fight terrorism by keeping life as usual as possible and ignoring the problems, while also holding true to principles and values.

That's the way you can fight things like separation of church and state. Real change is not made in the once-sacred halls of Congress but in the real America—the part of our nation that has not become jaded and corrupted with an "all is lost" attitude. Most of the "problems" facing America aren't real. Separation of church and state is one of them. This issue doesn't really invade the real America unless the ACLU has invaded one of the towns that dares to believe in God while at some public place.

We will, one day, see what's reality and what's mere perception when the politics of the big cities and the problems of Capitol Hill clash with America's heartland and the areas of our nation that have the "nerve" to be traditional.

This ongoing attack is almost an extreme part of our culture. Americans, unarguably, tend to compartmentalize certain elements of their lives with the workplace in one section, the family in one section, religious beliefs in one section, and another section for hobbies or other such things. Unfortunately, these compartments never merge. This is what happens with separation of church and state. We are unable to merge public offices with religious and moral beliefs. It's completely ridiculous—if not also a violation of the First Amendment right to freedom of religion.

A prime example of this would be when Attorney General John Ashcroft was facing the wolves of Senate confirmation. If you know anything about Ashcroft, you know he has shown deep religious and political beliefs. The Democratic Senate couldn't imagine him taking to his office with those beliefs and still acting responsibly. However, they have it all wrong. Judeo-Christian beliefs do not interfere with laws and the actions of government officials, but they reinforce them. Why else would the Constitution require a deeply religious and moral people? The Bible says to submit to the government and its laws. If anything can, these beliefs will be partly responsible for any return to a constitutional government in America.

After the terrorist attacks on America of September 11, 2001, we saw an amazing outcry from society. Wearing real, American-inspired clothing was the most popular; you could walk through a neighborhood and for miles see a line of American flags, church attendance rose, and Americans began to say, "God bless America," again.

Yet I wonder why God would have a reason to bless America. We have learned that God loves and cares about us all, but He also rewards those who turn to Him. Such would be the case when He blessed the founding of the nation. But we took a turn from our roots and have long ignored Him. This dangerous turn has taken a manifestation through the left-wing, anti-American, special-interest groups who wish to destroy the American culture, break down the American family, and chip away at the values of America that were once respectable.

During the arguments made in the Constitutional Convention, they had a hard time getting through the problems and making progress.

Benjamin Franklin took to the floor and said, "I have lived, Sir, a long time, and the longer I live, the more convincing proofs I see of this truth: 'that God governs in the affairs of man.' And if a sparrow cannot fall to the ground without His notice, is it probable that an empire can rise without His aid?"[18]

This empire rose with God's aid. This empire cannot continue without it, and to remove Him from all things in government would be nothing short of an implosive disaster.

Maybe it's too late. Maybe I'm a little too optimistic. Maybe I'm a radical. But I have faith in people. This nation has slowly but surely taken a turn from the liberal trend. Radio, the Internet, and books have, it seems, awakened the Sleeping Giant.

These political games, you know, are only kept alive by the people. Regardless of what the cynics say, people still have power. Maybe not on Capitol Hill or in the political powers of Washington, but we give those political machines the money. We give politicians their pay-checks. We support special interests. We pay taxes.

It may sound like rhetoric, but it's true when they say "people have the power." The Declaration of Independence clearly shows a fundamental and universal power that the people retain in any place, "when in the Course of human Events, it becomes necessary for one People to dissolve the Political Bands which have connected them with another, and to assume among the Powers of the Earth, the separate and equal Station to which the Laws of Nature and of Nature's God entitle them, a decent Respect to the Opinions of Mankind requires that they should declare the causes which impel them to the Separation."

It can change. But as with almost all the problems facing our free republic, it takes time, determination, and integrity.

Yes, ACLU, AU, NEA, NOW, PPFA, et al., you can attack to remove all things of God from public view, and you can attempt to demoralize this country, but you will never, ever silence the belief of traditional and American values in private and in public.

FURTHER READING

Books

- Gary T. Amos, *Defending the Declaration* (Brentwood, TN: Wolgemuth and Hyatt, 1989).
- David Barton, *Original Intent*, 3rd ed. (Aledo, TX: Wallbuilders, 2002).
- John Eidsomoe, *Christianity and the Constitution* (Grand Rapids: Baker, 1987).
- M. Stanton Evans, *The Theme Is Freedom* (Washington, DC: Regnery, 1994).
- William J. Federer, *America's God and Country Encyclopedia of Quotations* (Coppell, TX: Fame Publishing, 1994).
- Ellis Sandoz, ed., *Political Sermons of the American Founding Era* (Indianapolis: Liberty Fund, 1991).

Web Site

- www.wallbuilders.com

Sound Off

★ THE RIGHT CHOICE ★

10

The Founders Again

SECOND U.S. PRESIDENT JOHN ADAMS SAID, "OUR Constitution was made only for a moral and religious people. It is wholly inadequate to the government of any other."[1] Freedom and liberty can only be held safe by strong, mature, and responsible men and women who can stand up for their beliefs and not let pressure get the best of them when they are in the line of fire. The Founders of our great country knew this. They looked at the newly founded republic as a great experiment. Furthermore, with all their wisdom and intelligence, they also realized that the only way America could survive was through the responsibility of her citizens.

Without men living responsibly under it, the Constitution is little except a piece of paper—which is why John Adams brought up this point. Although there are exceptions, as a rule, religious men will follow the law of the land and submit to the dictates of the Constitution; a truly moral man would never intentionally break the law passed by Congress, much less break and distort the document upon which Congress rests, unless there were extraordinary reasons—such as his government behaving illegally and immorally.

Unfortunately, our people have elected more than a few immoral men to the highest seats in the land.

The negative aspect of electing people such as Bill Clinton to the presidency is total disregard for the Constitution of the United States. Besides the numerous affairs he had during his presidency, Clinton also used his Justice Department, under the control of Janet Reno, to cover his tail on countless criminal activities.[2]

Besides breaking the Constitution with numerous social programs, Franklin Delano Roosevelt attempted to unseat nearly an entire Supreme Court in order to allow his decisions and legislation. Present times and history have shown us that, in crises, elected "representatives" are able to trample on the Constitution and get legislation passed that destroys rights because the population allows them to do so.

These unconstitutional and un-American policies and programs are usually enacted because the population is simply uninformed and fearful, and the government is willing and ready to step in and "attempt" to erase that fear. If the American people decide to allow these sorts of people to take charge of the country, the next man down the line will see what others got away with and break the law more than the previous man. Therefore, it is not only the fault of President Roosevelt, although he is accountable for his actions; it is partly the fault of the American people for electing such a criminal. Feel-goodism, feelings, and emotion have gotten the best of too many generations and resulted in several losses for our republic.

Unfortunately, society has been served up revisionist history for some time. To set that right, we should look at what the Founders thought and how it applies to many of the pressing issues of our day—issues addressed in this book.

FREEDOM

The most recognized belief of the original intent of the Founders is simply freedom—liberty. Go no farther than Patrick Henry's exclamation: "Give me liberty, or give me death!" Fundamental to this freedom is the right of property; the Founders thought all citizens possessed the right of private ownership.

According to the First Article of the 1776 Virginia Declaration of Rights, "All men are by nature equally free and independent, and have certain inherent rights . . . namely, the enjoyment of life and liberty, with the means of acquiring and possessing property."

The reason that property is so highly thought of is that it's basic to freedom. "Without private property, government would own the churches, printing presses, and factories. Government would be able to dictate the practice of religion, speech, and employment, as it does under communism," says political scholar Thomas G. West.[3]

One area where property is obviously important is in speech. As West points out, if the government owns your pulpit, newspaper, or billboards, then who controls the speech? It's not you. Government already controls the airwaves, and wide disagreement with government policy or lively debates about it are not often heard on TV or radio.

This is dangerous. The free exchange of ideas and philosophies is quite possibly one of the main reasons America became the greatest country on the planet. However, many have taken this freedom and used it for ways to silence those who disagree with their point of view. As the cliché goes, "They want freedom of speech until you disagree with them."

This goes back to the point that the main way a free republic can survive is through maturity and responsibility. Unfortunately, the little maturity and responsibility that are left are far and few between.

Through responsibility and maturity comes a virtue of hearing one out, albeit you disagree with their point of view. However, that virtue has all but died in the organizations of the Left, such as the National Organization for Women, Planned Parenthood, the National Association for the Advancement of Colored People, and the National Education Association. Intolerance from the Left has muted free speech and stifled the free exchange of ideas—perhaps because if people were exposed to honest debates of the issues, they would reject liberal policies as unrealistic, unconstitutional, and occasionally idiotic.

Controlling speech and property has the twin end of destroying freedom and the individual's ability to live his life as he sees fit. The core reason that communism, socialism, and a command economy do not work is the simple fact that you can't sell an object that you yourself do not own. Unlike in a market economy, a communist market cannot produce economic growth because its citizens cannot trade, buy, sell, take out a loan, or lend. A person cannot have collateral to take out a loan if the person doesn't own his or her belongings. While we look at an entire economy failing because of these policies, we sometimes fail to remember that the economy is just millions of people—millions of people robbed of their freedom. And the threat is getting worse here in the U.S.

Government is, inch by inch, making its way into the private sector by way of wealth redistribution, subsidies, and "relief" money. Wealth redistribution can be seen through social welfare programs that were unfortunately created by Franklin Delano Roosevelt. While the thought may be nice and everything looks good when it's down on paper, the government taking money from my pocket to put in someone else's will solve nothing in the long term.

Subsidies for corporations and farms are another form of legalized theft. Although aid for farms may be necessary in order to sustain small farms, it is, again, not helping anyone in the long term. If, for example, government aid was cut off to farmers, many small farms would be lost, but large farms would replace them. This is to say that times will not always be smooth, but the free market and the market economy will eventually work itself out, and government will have nothing to do with it.

The alternative is a failed system where people live like serfs instead of free men.

FAITH

From the Pilgrims and Puritans to the preachers of the Revolution, America's founding is swimming in faith. Thanks to the ACLU and others, however, the religious imprint on America is harder and harder to see.

The so-called separation of church and state has been used as a wedge to drive religion out of public life. Supposedly, this idea is found in the First Amendment. But as we found in the previous chapter, that idea is rubbish. The First Amendment simply states, "Congress shall make no law respecting an establishment of religion, or prohibiting the free exercise thereof; or abridging the freedom of speech, or of the press; or the right of the people peaceably to assemble, and to petition the government for a redress of grievances." I don't see the word *separation* there once, do you? Obviously not.

Many "advocacy" groups have hijacked the words of Thomas Jefferson and have gone on a crusade to remove the word *God* and all things pertaining to religion from government.

But what were the Founders thinking to start with?

James Madison, the father of the Constitution, said, "We have staked the whole future of American civilization not upon the power of government, far from it. We have staked the future of all of our political institutions upon the capacity of mankind for self-government—upon the capacity of each and all of us to govern ourselves, to control ourselves, to sustain ourselves according to the ten commandments of God."[4]

Freedom requires responsibility or it just becomes licentiousness; faith and morality provide that needed backbone. In his Farewell Address, George Washington said, "Of all the dispositions and habits which lead to political prosperity, Religion and morality are indispensable supports," adding that virtue "is a necessary spring of popular government."

During the Constitutional Convention, the delegates prayed to God for His aid in crafting the new government. Additionally, every time Congress begins session, there is a prayer—this tradition was started by the first Congress.

By looking at a few quotes—which are the tip of the iceberg—we can see that the Founders' original intent didn't call for a great "separation" between all things in the church and all things in government.

Most of them were Christians whose beliefs influenced their policies and decisions. Although the Founders didn't call for or believe in a national and official religion, the majority of them were Christians and believed in Judeo-Christian values. This language is evident all through the founding documents.

The great danger of liberal organizations trying to de-Christianize America is that our freedom goes out the window when our faith does.

LIFE

One of the reasons the Founders' belief in God is so important is that, as the Declaration of Independence states it, rights are granted by God and are inalienable because of it. Rights cannot be taken by government; they are from God, and only He can remove them. One such inalienable right listed in the Declaration is the right to life.

Unlike nations such as Communist China, this country was founded on the belief that Americans shouldn't be afraid for their lives at every waking moment. While the Founders would probably have never imagined it would come this far, this right also protects the right of the unborn. In even more extremes, it also includes the right to give birth to a child and not be coerced by population control measures. Both of which are realities in China, where couples are not allowed more than one child.

But breaches of the right to life happen all over America in a less openly tyrannical sort of way.

The Declaration of Independence doesn't say, "We hold these Truths to be self-evident, that all Men—except the helpless unborn—are created equal, that they are endowed by their Creator with certain unalienable Rights, that among these are Life, Liberty and the Pursuit of Happiness." But that's precisely what the practice of abortion assumes is true.

Many groups have hijacked the word *freedom* to their own advantage: "the freedom to choose." Nevertheless, the countless unborn children obviously didn't have the right to choose life because they were simply inconvenient.

The "right" to abort has made top placement on the distortion of "freedom" list. Do you really think our Founders—who risked the burning of their houses, the killing of their families, and certain death by Great Britain—did what they did for our "right" to kill the unborn? Certainly not.

In this issue, many have hidden behind and stirred up a debate about when the baby becomes life: at conception, three months old, six months old, or the first breath. One could debate on this for hours and not create any progress. On the other hand, the whole debate seems to be a smoke screen. It doesn't matter when life begins. What does matter is that if it weren't for abortions, about 40 million more lives would be in the world today.

What would the Founders say about abortion? Concerning the nature of rights and the responsibility of government, the Declaration goes on to state, "That to secure these Rights, Governments are instituted among Men, deriving their just Powers from the Consent of the Governed, that whenever any Form of Government becomes destructive of these Ends, it is the Right of the People to alter or to abolish it."

EQUALITY

Given the American people seem so contented with denying so many the right to life, some may miss the importance of this next statement: the Constitution requires that a right given to one must be given to all. A person cannot be more important than the next; everyone stands equally before the law. In 1794, Timothy Ford wrote that, while people possessed "inequality of condition," nature "created all men free and equal in their rights."[5]

Many movements in America are working to undermine this principle, including slavery reparations and homosexual marriage.

Reparations deny equality before the law because they force American taxpayers to pay for crimes they haven't committed, while modern-day blacks, who were never slaves, are granted special favors as if they had been.

The "homosexual rights" movement has tried to use this idea to its own advantage. By using the rule that government is to remain un-biased, many lobby the government to allow for homosexual "mar-riages" and the like. The argument is pretty simple: if you give certain rights and privileges to someone, you have to give them to all. Armed with that basic idea, many groups have successfully fought for legal status of homosexual "marriages."

However, while the principle is right, the application is miles off. No definitive and documented evidence has been presented that shows homosexuality is a genetic trait. Therefore, no special rights, privileges, and legal status should be granted to homosexual "marriages." Marriage is between men and women; if homosexuals want to marry outside their sex, no one is stopping them.

GOVERNMENT

Although Jefferson and Madison disagreed on certain powers of the federal government, as a rule, most of the first patriots agreed and believed in a limited and nonintrusive government. The present gov-ernment, however, is seemingly unlimited as it only grows and becomes more intrusive.

The Fourth Amendment of the Constitution states, "The right of the people to be secure in their persons, houses, papers, and effects, against unreasonable searches and seizures, shall not be violated, and no warrants shall issue, but upon probable cause, supported by oath or affirmation, and particularly describing the place to be searched, and the persons or things to be seized."

However, many in government wish to expand the authority of their employer by allowing them to search persons, houses, papers, and effects without a proper warrant. In major cities across the country, the local police are implementing huge networks of security cameras in subways, schools, government buildings, streets, and other public places. Such an idea caused a major stir in Washington, D.C., in 2002.[6]

Fear is a very strong tool and it can be a great motivator—for better or for worse. Many government officials harnessed the fear that the terrorist attacks on September 11 created, and under the banner of "security," they successfully restricted the freedoms of Americans.

In terms of government growth, you can see the state overstepping its bounds every day.

What do black reparations, federal farm legislation, Native American payouts, and the September 11 recovery all have in common? Answer: the evolution of a free democratic-republic into a socialist nation. In a socialist nation, one of the key factors—which is an essential component and cornerstone of socialism—is the redistributing from among the people of that nation, coordinated by the government.

The payouts of September 11 by charities were enormous, but even bigger and unprecedented were the payouts by the U.S. government, which may become a big problem for our nation. Now that the precedent has been established for the payout of government money to victims of attacks, greed will inevitably take over—and few people in their right minds would turn down $1 million from the government.

I happen to have Native American blood in my veins, as do my siblings, mother, grandfather, and up the line. It's beside the point, of course, that the imprisoning, murder, misplacement, and slaughtering of Native Americans have no relevant effect on my life. So, I'm assuming my family and many other families could become fairly wealthy if we successfully rallied support in Congress for a payout to those who have Native American blood.

The same idea is being put into motion for blacks. With the likes of Al Sharpton and Jesse Jackson, support is gathering for the United

States government to hand out money to African-Americans—"reparations."

Unfortunately, the payout program for attacks is making its way to Oklahoma, where I live. Senators from Oklahoma proposed a $300 million payout to the victims of the Oklahoma City bombing—nearly $2 million a person.[7]

It's as if anything bad that happens on this government's watch is the direct fault of that government—and ultimately, the American people. Therefore, because the guy next door got a $1 million check as a victim of the OKC bombing, the lady down the road wants a check because she was in a car wreck last week.

One of the largest farm bills, which was passed by Congress in May 2002, called for spending $200 billion in subsidies for farms across ten years.

With the farm bill, as with all the examples given, the government is taking my money and giving it to someone else. That's just as if I brought a gun into a crowded room and demanded $1,000 from everyone to help my friend start a business. Why is it government doesn't get charged with theft? As with any government subsidies, reparations, and welfare programs, they are taking from my pocket and your pocket to give to someone else. However, the government has made its theft—the redistributing of wealth—legalized.

Every time you turn around, someone is demanding more and more money for something. Ironically, some of the people who are calling for payouts from these disasters are from the crowd that is always calling for "fiscal discipline." You can't have it both ways, folks.

While the touchy-feely, soft, and cuddly direction will feel good and make us all happy inside for the time being, the road we're heading down is sheer lunacy. In a society where a government redistributes wealth, it always causes divisiveness. The Robin Hood approach will never work. If these plans go into effect, soon there won't be enough money to take from—you can only tax public citizens so much. No wonder we will never pay back the national debt; the government continues to grow, and the money does not. The extreme redistribution of wealth is not economically feasible.

Government has invaded the realm of charities, but unlike private charities, it is demanding money by force and not allowing free will to be established so citizens can contribute to the charities that they wish.

Instead of relying on government to make things right, communities should, as they have before government got in the picture, come together and help each other take care of their problems by generosity and free will.

"The sacred fire of liberty and the destiny of the republican model of government are justly considered," President George Washington said in his First Inaugural Address, "as deeply, perhaps finally, staked on the experiment entrusted to the hands of the American people."[8] As expressed in his Inaugural Address, George Washington and many other Founders believed that the life of America was an experiment, and the results of that experiment have rested in the hands of the American people.

Those responsibilities include not letting charismatic politicians get the best of the voters and not letting emotion stand in the way of values and principles. However, it is unfortunate that in the past years, emotion has allowed for the electing of crooks.

Public opinion unarguably controls a lot of the workings of our nation. And because public opinion controls the inner workings of government, it has led to many problems facing the nation.

However, it is not all the citizens' fault. Rather, it is also the fault of elected officials who submit to the power of public opinion, even though they realize the consequences involved.

The key issue at hand is that of democracy destroying our once great nation. Alexander Tytler wrote, "A democracy cannot exist as a permanent form of government. It can only exist until the voters discover that they can vote themselves largesse from the public treasury."[9]

The popular mind-set of current politicians is to make a career out of being an elected official. Just look at Senator Byrd. With this found love of being elected and reelected, it creates a pathway for special-interest groups to demand money for attacks, wrecks, natural disasters, or other forms of "largesse." Therefore, through this democratic system, everyone gets what they want for the time being.

However, Alexander Tytler went on to write, "The majority always votes for the candidates promising them the most benefits from the public treasury, with the result that democracy always collapses over loose fiscal policy, always followed by dictatorship."[10]

As in the case of government handouts, payouts, and federal "charities," the one losing is the posterity of this society because when doing this, government either must raise taxes or go bankrupt.

On the other hand, I believe there is still a gleam of hope left to restore our fallen republic. By surveying the current landscape of America, we can see that it doesn't line up or even compare to the vision of the Founders. And because it doesn't line up with their views and beliefs, our nation is heading toward an all-out cliff of destruction. Therefore, work must be done to help restore it—and the changes required are quite drastic.

Using the power of public education to an advantage, the teaching of the state constitutions, the Declaration of Independence, the United States Constitution, and other historical documents will help many children realize the inner workings of our government and see when officials step out of bounds. By knowing the inner workings of the government, a society will be more inclined to ask the right questions of government and remain more vigilant when watching constitutional and political issues.

Surely, the only way our once great country can survive and begin the restoration process is to work toward a more informed and intelligent society. Politicians across the country spread disinformation in politics and campaigns, but the citizens take it as truth. On the economy, for instance, many liberal Democrats claim that higher taxes are good for the economy and tax breaks are bad for the economy. Why we still have debates on this is beyond me. The simple economic rule states that the cheaper a product is, the more likely it is to be bought, and the more money a person has, the more likely it is that he or she will buy a product. Therefore, if the government can allow for cheaper goods and money in the hands of the consumer by way of a tax break, it will bring about nothing but economic growth—because economic growth will not be brought about by subsidies and the redistributing of wealth.

The biggest aspect of responsibility that the Founders stressed was the need for proper education. Education in God, education in the proper form of government, but most important, education in how to keep and preserve freedom.

EDUCATION

The single most compelling reason for the failing of the American experiment is laid at the feet of public education. Government-run public schools have had their chance. For over one hundred years, schools have been operated publicly by the government, and from the beginning, it has been going downhill alongside the intelligence of America.

Education is the passing, one generation to another, of the knowledge and skills required for a people's survival and advancement. But thanks to the failure of government schools, this transmission of information has been slowed or virtually stopped.

The simple fact is that the more intelligent and experienced a society can be, the better. The public school system is not delivering that, and it cannot be changed in a bigger and better bill introduced in the Senate. On the contrary, it must be fixed by individuals, home-schooling, local private social programs, and outside reform because the government cannot and will not be able to successfully reform the education system.

What's at stake here is our very republic.

We need the Founders again. We need their vision, their view of politics and society. If a school system can successfully teach the founding documents and the original intent of the Founders, an upcoming society will be well grounded in the way government is supposed to work.

If you've read the whole book and made it this far, or if you just skipped to the end, one of the main things emphasized is exactly what Abraham Lincoln, despite his other actions, said: "The philosophy of the schoolroom in one generation will be the philosophy of the government in the next." Therefore, our philosophy in the schoolroom must be an American philosophy.

RESPONSIBILITY

Ultimately, the only way our nation has the possibility of being saved is if selfishness is replaced by responsibility—and the only way that can be done is if we instill it into our young men and women.

The freedom that America was founded upon was not the freedom to kill unborn baby children, and it was not the freedom to shred them up as they take their first breath. The freedom that America was founded on was not the freedom to brainwash our children into secular humanism. It also was not founded to allow social persecution against all those who believe in absolute morality and truth.

Moreover, this freedom did not allow a body to prevent these things to occur by way of legislation, but it allowed for the citizens of the United States to uphold the greatest and utmost individual responsibility in order to prevent this occurrence.

The main reason America was created was for a better life for the posterity of our Founders. The blood, sweat, tears, and death were not just for themselves, but they acted selflessly in an effort to allow freedom to survive for generations to come.

FURTHER READING

Books

- M. Stanton Evans, *The Theme Is Freedom* (Washington, DC: Regnery, 1994).

- Joseph Farah, *Taking America Back* (Nashville: WND Books, 2002).

- George Grant, *The Patriot's Handbook* (Nashville: Cumberland, 2000).

- Sean Hannity, *Let Freedom Ring: Winning the War of Liberty Over Liberalism* (New York: Harper, 2002).

- G. Gordon Liddy, *When I Was a Kid, This Was a Free Country* (Washington, DC: Regnery, 2002).

- Catherine Millard, *The Rewriting of American History* (Camp Hill: Horizon Books, 1991).

- Thomas G. West, *Vindicating the Founders* (New York: Rowman and Littlefield, 1997).

- Jeffrey St. John, *Constitutional Journal: A Correspondent's Report From the Convention of 1787* (Ottawa: Jameson Books, 1987).

Web Sites

- www.wallbuilders.com
- www.declaration.net
- www.face.net
- www.achipa.com

CONCLUSION

Which Is the Greatest Generation?

OUR NATION IS FACING MANY PROBLEMS IN THIS DAY AND age. I myself have struggled with whether to give up hope or continue to hold out a guarded optimism and belief that one day America will return to its intention and purpose.

I have come to the conclusion that there is hope for freedom and conservatism in America. The obvious opportunities that this generation of conservatives have are vast. We have the Internet, radio, and a growing effort of communication and organization. All these things will allow constitutionalism to gain power in mainstream American.

The reason to hold out hope is that these options weren't available to previous generations. The Internet as we know it has only been around for a handful of years; mainstream talk radio has only been around for a little over a decade. Conservative organizations are just now getting a grasp on the organizing and networking that made the Left successful.

There is reason to have hope, and it is not in vain. However, a great amount of work must be done, and we must handle it the right way. This generation, my generation, has the chance of becoming the true "greatest generation."

The so-called greatest generation did their part in defending our nation from the external threats of Europe and the evils of the Nazi

Empire, and they kept our nation alive during the tough times. Yet as Walter E. Williams points out, they failed to uphold the Constitution at home.[1] Worse, they failed to educate their children in the ideals of America and the way to internally preserve our nation. The result of this folly: a great disconnect between previous generations' love and appreciation of the Constitution and our present dislike and hatred for it.

On the other hand, my generation—generation Y or whatever they call us—is in a similar spot. We are in the position to defend our nation against the external threats of terrorism, but we need to defend our nation against the internal threats of liberalism and socialism. Education is the key.

It's a do-or-die situation. The mantle has been dropped before, but it must not be dropped again. We're at a crossroads, and we have to follow through. If the coming generation is worse or equal to the baby boomers and Gen X, we're in deep trouble. The irresponsibility and immaturity of those generations boggle the mind. Not to bash or lecture anyone, but look at the state of our nation now. Who has been in charge of it? Those generations.

Therefore, support, encourage, and take part in the up-and-coming generation, so hopefully this one can be the American generation we need. It will take hard work, a lot of blood, a lot of sweat, and many tears. We can do it, but we must not and cannot forget the ideals and the values of our nation. Otherwise, America is no different from any other nation—these values and ideas are the only hope for freedom. You may take your pick of the United Socialist States of America, but the old America works for me.

APPENDIX

Young Activists

THE WAYS FOR YOUNG PEOPLE TO BECOME INVOLVED IN the political process are enormous and needed. However, those ways are not always encouraged or known. Therefore, here is a list of ten ways teens (and in some ways, adults) can have the opportunity to become involved:

1. JOIN OR FORM A COMMUNITY POLITICAL GROUP

Examples of the success of such things are two local groups I am associated with. The first would be the local Young Republicans affiliate. The group meets once a month at the local library or a café to address political issues and listen to politicians and activists speak. Much is gained, and it allows you to learn how to speak in public as well as become involved in local, state, and even national politics.

The other, the Oklahoma Conservative Political Action Committee, has hosted such guests as Alan Keyes, David Barton, Steve Largent, and countless other politicians, scholars, and activists. In addition to having notable speakers, the group awards donations to candidates based on their score in its Conservative Index and how they speak, as well as being the authority on what legislation is reviewed for the state.

Both these groups were formed by only a few people, but have grown to a large membership and have become very influential in state and local politics in Oklahoma.

Such a group allows for a great way to promote conservative ideas, an avenue to highlight local and state events that may be of interest, support candidates for political office, shed light on issues concerning communities and the political arena, and a vehicle for like-minded people to meet and share the same ideas and goals, and fight for conservatism and American ideas.

2. BECOME INVOLVED WITH LEGISLATIVE OFFICIALS

There are programs in local communities known as "shadow" programs. These programs are usually presented by the local city council or other legislative body and sponsor a teen to match up him or her to a public official. The official will sponsor a young person for a period of time by letting him or her in on the inner workings of legislation and the happenings of office.

This, obviously, is for young people, but definitely something for parents to check out for their child or a teen to look into. Such a program will help anyone learn more about the local political process.

3. PAGING

Get in touch with your state senator or representative, and find out about paging for the legislature. This is much like the "shadow" program, but you work by doing chores for the representative or senator in the state legislature while it is in session—a perfect way to learn about the legislative system.

4. COMMUNICATION IN WRITING

One of the most powerful ways to communicate a belief, viewpoint, or agenda is through the written word. These thoughts can then be published and delivered to the masses, causing potentially huge influence. This, of course, depends on the size of readership, but since the invention of the Gutenberg press, a revolution in delivery of news and information began.

Now, we have such venues as daily state and national newspapers for political discourse and information. This allows for an opportunity to write letters to the editor and commentary that can shape viewpoints, allow for political discussion, and possibly change opinions.

In addition, getting your thoughts and ideas into public view can stimulate and encourage others who have the same values.

5. NEWSLETTERS

Another way to become influential at a community, state, or possibly national level is to create a newspaper or newsletter. Not only is this a way to publish crucial information on political and current events, but a way to get announcements and information on coming events. Whether it be delivered through the United States mail service or electronically through e-mail, a newsletter can be sent to the masses and assume a key role in politics and the happenings of government.

In my state of Oklahoma, the Oklahoma Family Policy Council sends a statewide, quarterly newsletter called *The Oklahoma Citizen.* The newsletter "gives readers news they can use about state and national issues and events affecting their homes and families."

There is also a quarterly newspaper that has grown in Oklahoma since 1979 called the *Oklahoma Constitution.* The newspaper, founded by four politically active conservatives, produced the first issue in February 1979, but since then, it has grown to enormous heights as the state authority on the Conservative Index, as well as publishing top-of-the-line conservative commentary on state and national issues.

These are two examples of a way to become influential in local, state, and national politics.

Still, such a tool can also be used to mentor and help young people to get into the political arena by generating interest. This element is very powerful. Using it, you can teach teens and adults alike about rights that we have from God protected by the Constitution. It can also be used to promote conservative ideas, traditional values, promote free and independent thought, and express a love of country the way Ronald Reagan did.

6. INTERNET

Another tool in a way of getting involved in and allowing for political activism and awareness is through none other than the greatest form of communication: the Internet.

Through the success stories of Web sites that have been started by one or two people, you can see the ability and opportunity to become influential in the political process of America.

Free Republic is one of them. No, I am not talking about our nation, but an Internet forum at FreeRepublic.com. The Web site was started by a single man to create an alternative for Internet-accessible conservatives. Well, this alternative worked. The Free Republic monster has grown to an amazing height by organizing activism chapters across the nation, planning protests, and boasting nearly 80,000 registered "Freepers."

WorldNetDaily, with which I have been fortunate enough to be a part, has also made waves across the Internet and into the vibe of the political and news-making arena. Starting in 1997 as a small Web site updated daily by Joseph and Elizabeth Farah, it has grown to break many national and international news stories, has added dozens of political opinion columnists, and WorldNetDaily.com brags of 2.5 million different viewers visiting the site each month.

For younger people, CPI News would be a good example of what young people can accomplish on the Internet. The Web site, CPINews.net, was founded by two homeschooled brothers, Daniel and Nathan McClintock, one evening on the computers in their room. The idea was to shine light on the conservative issues of the day, but it has grown into a full-blown news service with a growing list of contributors.

That's just a tiny tip of a huge iceberg. You also have DrudgeReport.com, TownHall.com, CaptoVeritas.com, EnterStage Right.com, NationalReview.com, JewishWorldReview.com, CNS News.com, InstaPundit.com, YConservatives.com, FrontPage Mag.com, NewsMax.com, WeeklyStandard.com, OpinionJournal.com, and the list goes on and on (and on).

It's obvious that conservatives have started to fight back with thoughtful, reasoned, and logical campaigns against the monster of liberalism that has monopolized cable, local television networks, newspapers, entertainment, and colleges across the nation. Furthermore, constitutionalists continue to fight through two mediums: the Internet and radio. Therefore, another way to join this fight and get involved is by joining the Internet and technology revolution.

7. VOLUNTEERING

In order to become involved in politics, you need experience and knowledge. There are two types of knowledge: knowledge from experience and knowledge from secondhand experiences, stories, and books. Both are equally valuable, but as indicated by the criticism I receive (and I get quite a bit), knowledge from experience is more valuable to the critics. Yet if your opinions are true, just, and right, it doesn't matter how you get to those conclusions, though some may and probably do disagree.

However, in order to receive knowledge and experience in politics, volunteering is one of the greatest ways to do that. And in the political arena, finding places and campaigns to volunteer for is quite possibly the easiest thing to do. Local, state, and national candidates will welcome anyone with open arms to do nearly any job that helps the campaign. From calling possible voters, manning phones, putting out signs, to going door to door, helping to organize rallies, and doing miscellaneous chores, it's not hard to find a position that works for you.

8. BOOK KNOWLEDGE

No, you're not being quizzed on the content of this book. I'm talking about the knowledge gained by reading and taking in secondhand accounts of the past. This is, obviously, the main way to learn about the past.

I, for example, write much in this book and in my columns on the ideas and values of Ronald Reagan, although I didn't live during the years of his administration. I was coming into this world as he headed out of the White House. Still, I have read many books on the ideas of Reagan, such as a book filled with his radio addresses, a book of quotes, as well as other details on his life. Because of that, I consider myself well versed in the values of the Reagan Revolution.

Furthermore, this is the way to ground yourself in debate and opinions. The only way your opinion is going to be taken seriously is if you can defend it logically with evidence and the facts of history. Therefore, another way to be influential is to simply read biographies, history books, and whatever you can get your hands on.

9. NETWORKING

Networking, as in befriending and getting acquainted with people, is a key part of involvement in politics. Anyone who has been politically active can testify to this. In order to get things done, you must have a lot of friends and acquaintances who can help you out.

The items on this list of ideas generally flow and go together, as networking can be done through joining local political action committees or other such organizations. Yet attending speaking events and political rallies can also be another way.

However you do it, knowing your way around the landscape of politics is necessary if you ever plan on getting anything done. But not to worry, most will welcome you with open arms because it is most always a mutual relationship of give-and-take.

10. STAYING INFORMED

The key to defending conservatism is merely being informed about the debate topic. Easier said than done, but the best way is to simply follow the news and the happenings on Capitol Hill. Simple because it's easier now than ever to be and stay informed—with the cable news choices, newspapers, the popularity of radio, the Internet, and (if you dare) the evening news. To have news and information, all it takes is a click of a mouse, a turn of the dial, or a change of the channel.

GET THE THINKING

While the above steps help in the practical sense, we need grounding in the ideological arena as well. It is crucial that young people learn the principles of conservatism. Some have caught on to that and provide resources for young conservatives.

There are many organizations dedicated to mentoring, arming, and encouraging high school and college students. Those organizations must be commended. Here are two programs that are available to most teens and/or college students.

The first group is one of the most popular and biggest advocates for young conservatives in the country. If you have done any searching or research on the field of conservative mentoring groups, you are bound to have heard of this organization. The Young America's Foundation was founded to ensure that "increasing numbers of young Americans understand and are inspired by the ideas of individual freedom, a strong national defense, free enterprise, and traditional values," as the group's Web site (www.yaf.org) states.

The organization has annual conferences for high schoolers and college students where they receive training and hear influential and famous conservatives speak. The organization also has regional conferences at different times of the year, along with a speakers bureau that has a long list of conservative speakers who go on college tours throughout the year.

"We seek to expose students to conservative principles and bring balance to the campus debate," the group says. "Young America's Foundation alleviates the isolation so many young conservatives face by providing them with the tools to defend their beliefs and by creating a network of support for like-minded students."

Another organization dedicated to the education of teenagers is Teen Pact. This is a national Christian organization that has programs in nearly every state. The program takes attendants to the state legislature in teaching them how it works, parliamentary procedure, learning their way around the Capitol, morning Bible devotions, and quite a bit more.

The aim of Teen Pact is to educate. As the group's Web site (www.teenpact.com) describes the experience, "You can't go into a Legislature anywhere in the country and not be inundated with paper: bills, amendments, disclosures, rosters, code sections, committee reports. They all seem so confusing at first. Students leave the Capitol with a better idea of the importance of each document and how they can use them as citizens for the rest of their lives."

Both these programs support and inspire the youth of America and work for a better future. It is a great example of where conservatives should be in accepting young conservatives into the political arena.

ENCOURAGING YOUTH

The statement can be made that young people should not only be allowed to become involved in the political process of America, but should be encouraged, not shunned.

The future of the nation is being raised in the public education system, so if you look at the standards of government schools in comparison to the required leadership and goals in public offices, the next generation of leaders is in need of prayer.

Therefore, to counter the near indoctrination in government education, private organizations must be formed, mentor groups must be formed, and advocacy groups must be formed with not a particular partisan view in mind, but a dedication to teaching the real American principles that are all but lost in today's society. The sense of the way our nation was intended to operate must return to the pulse of the country.

This is not necessarily about a drive for conservative teenagers to have a shot at political involvement, but an education for teenagers that will enable them to take the reins of the nation, knowing their goals and what is right.

This generic idea has been recognized by many and some have had the guts to push their way into the legislative bodies to get real American education into the schools, but the fact is, the hog of government education is not going to commit suicide.

The We the People Foundation, for instance, is an organization that has sponsored an initiative titled "Operation Enduring Patriotism." The organization, based out of New York, has gathered volunteers from all fifty states to contact their state representatives in an effort to get legislation passed in all states that would require an in-depth teaching of the United States Constitution, Declaration of Independence, and the state constitution, as well as observing special patriotic holidays and teaching patriotism and citizenship.

This particular initiative has become successful in many states, but some have not been so lucky, as the efforts of Dr. David Yeagley attest. Being a successful columnist and professor, he had the ability to push for a patriotism bill in Oklahoma. The bill would mandate the observance of Veterans Day, the posting of patriotic and religious documents, a daily moment of silence, and a daily flag salute. The good news is that the legislation passed the Oklahoma House of Representatives in the spring of 2002, in a vote of 99-0. However,

Oklahoma's Senate Education Committee chairwoman killed the bill, saying, "This bill was not about patriotism, this bill was about religion, and God doesn't need our help."[1]

Unfortunately, this is the way it has gone for many bills and many programs intended to save the republic, but were forced down the hill by the anti-American liberals that have been destroying our nation for over one hundred years.

A role of youth in politics and news of the day doesn't put kids on an equal plane with adults and elders. Furthermore, it doesn't remotely mean that kids and teenagers should be making the decisions for the local, state, or national levels, and allowing a young base of participation doesn't mean teens and adults are peers.

Even the Bible clearly states that we should treat our elders with respect. Therefore, elders are in authority over the rest. And that's a good thing. The responsibility and maturity needed for public office and crucial decisions seem to come with age and experience. This, however, is different from giving opinions.

You rarely, if ever, see a public official criticize political pundits for their opinions, but it's always the other way around. It's apparent why. The opinion of the Senate Majority Leader actually shapes politics and life in America, but the opinion of, say, Michelle Malkin or Ann Coulter, for instance, doesn't, unless the ideas are applied by someone in power.

An opinion is an opinion. That's it. It's nothing but a viewpoint from one person in a world of billions. It doesn't mean that I'm making policy changes for the United States when I write a column. It doesn't mean that I, Kyle Williams, am dictator of the world, bent on being a "religious radical." You can either take my opinion or leave it. Although, for now, people are taking my opinions, I stop giving them if that ends. It's a simple concept.

The opinions of teenagers should not be feared or pushed back. Although by no means should children have a corner of any market or rule anything, I should have my say on things. Beyond that, the rulers of this nation can decide what to do and either take my opinion or leave it. After all, this free speech thing we have isn't here for nothing.

The crucial step for America will be when the younger generation takes its opinions and makes law based on them. Then America will either become freer or drift farther into socialism and dependency on government.

FURTHER READING

Books

- Chuck Crismier, *Renewing the Soul of America* (Richmond, VA: Elijah Books, 2002).
- Dinesh D'Souza, *Letters to a Young Conservative* (New York: Basic Books, 2002).
- Steve Davis, Larry Elin, and Grant Reeher, *Click On Democracy: The Internet's Power to Change Political Apathy into Civic Action* (Cambridge, MA: Westview Press, 2002).
- Rush Limbaugh, *See, I Told You So* (New York: Pocket Books, 1993).
- Rush Limbaugh, *The Way Things Ought to Be* (New York: Pocket Books, 1992).

Web Sites

- www.teenpact.org
- www.yaf.org
- www.yconservatives.com
- www.captoveritas.com

NOTES

Chapter 1: Attacking the Family

1. American Humanist Association, *Humanist Manifesto I*, posted on-line at www.americanhumanist.org/about/manifesto1.html.

2. John A. Stormer, *None Dare Call It Education* (Florissant, MO: Liberty Bell Press, 1998), viii.

3. Wade F. Horn, Richard O. Weinhert, Alan Hawkins, and Thomas K. Sylvester, "Fatherhood & TV: An Evolution Report," National Fatherhood Initiative, spring 2000.

4. *O'Reilly Factor*, FOX News, 3 March 2002.

5. Jon Dougherty, "Sex Doesn't Sell?" WorldNetDaily.com, 22 April 2002.

6. Dr. Lynda Madison, "R-Rated Movies Lead to R-Rated Behavior," *Dr. Laura Perspective*, August 2002.

7. Media General/Associated Press Poll, #26, 5–13 May 1989.

8. "Sex Smarts," *Seventeen*, ongoing column posted on-line at www.seventeen.com/sexbody/sexsmarts/sexsmarts14.html.

9. David Keeps, interview with Alyson Hannigan, *Teen People*, 7 June 2002.

Chapter 2: Intolerance to the Extreme

1. National Education Association, Resolutions, Section B-31 (1981, 2001).

2. Matt Drudge, "Belafonte Slams Colin Powell as Race Sellout," *Drudge Report*, 8 October 2002.

3. "Jesse Joins Belafonte in Powell Attack," *New York Daily News*, 22 October 2002.

4. "Media Ignores Polls Showing Pro-Life Majorities," *National Review*, 23 August 2001.

5. "Familiar Routine of Scaring Seniors," *Washington Times*, 16 June 2002.

6. "GOP Objects to Social Security E-Mails," *Washington Post*, 4 October 2002.

7. "Have They No Shame?" *60 Plus Press Release*, 10 October 2002.

8. Report of the National Education Association Task Force on Sexual Orientation, 8 February 2002, Section A-1.

9. *60 Minutes*, CBS News, 20 October 2002.

10. Action Alert, "Demand That CBS and 60 Minutes Provide Responsible Reporting and Commentary," NOW, 25 October 2002.

Chapter 3: Media Bias

1. *Larry King Live*, CNN, 13 September 2002.

2. *Larry King Live*, CNN, 10 April 2002.

3. MSNBC ad, ran in *Wall Street Journal*, 15 July 2002.

4. Mark Jurkowitz, *Boston Globe*, 17 January 2002.

5. *Donahue*, MSNBC, 25 July 2002.

6. *CBS Evening News*, CBS, Dan Rather, 15 April 2002.

7. *CBS Early Show*, CBS, 2 December 2001.

8. *ABC World News Tonight*, ABC, 4 December 2001.

9. *NBC Nightly News*, NBC, 4 December 2001.

10. *Inside Politics*, CNN, 29 October 1996.

11. *Inside Politics*, CNN, 10 July 2002.

12. *CBS Evening News*, CBS, 6 December 1996.

13. *CBS Evening News*, CBS, 10 July 2002.

14. *ABC World News Tonight*, ABC, 27 August 2001.

15. *ABC World News Tonight*, ABC, 10 July 2002.

16. *NBC Nightly News*, NBC, 19 December 2001.

17. Ibid.

18. *NBC Nightly News*, NBC, 10 July 2002.

19. Ibid.

20. Matt Drudge, "Public Relations Debacle After Sen. Hillary Jeered and Booed by Heroes," *Drudge Report*, 21 October 2001.

21. American Society of Newspaper Editors, *The Newspaper Journalists of the 90s*, 1997.

22. Kaiser Family Foundation, National Survey of the Role of Polls in Policymaking, 2001.

23. *NBC Nightly News*, NBC, 8 May 2002.

24. Ibid.

25. *ABC World News Tonight*, ABC, 20 March 2002.

26. Ibid.

27. "Dan Rather: Bush Issued Bogus Terror Alert to Cover Up 9-11 Bungle," Newsmax.com, 22 May 2002.

28. National Public Radio, Morning Edition, David Kestenbaum, 22 January 2002.

29. Evelyn Neives, "In Twin Speeches, Bush and Cheney Vow to Fight Fraud," *New York Times*, 8 August 2002.

30. "Corrections," third correction, *New York Times*, 15 August 2002.

Chapter 4: A Liberal Education

1. Jessica Brice, "More Than 50 Percent of Students Fail High-stakes Graduation Test," *San Diego Union Tribune*, 30 September 2002.

2. "Colleges Told to Ignore Test Scores," ABCNews.com, 7 November 2002.

3. "N.C. Education Officials Throw Out Low Writing Scores, Say Test to Blame," Associated Press, TBO.com, 11 July 2002.

4. Stormer, *None Dare Call It Education*, viii.

5. Barbara Curtis, "(Gay) School Days," *Citizen*, July 2001.

Chapter 5: Alternative Learning

1. "Kindergartner's Stripper-Mom in Church-School Flap," WorldNetDaily.com, 16 May 2002.

2. Charter School Highlights and Statistics, Center for Education Reform, fall 2002, posted on-line at www.edreform.com/pubs/chglance.htm.

3. "Charter School Survey," Center for Education Reform, 1996–1997.

4. Associated Press, "Charter Students' Math, Reading Skills Lag Public School Peers," *USA Today*, 3 September 2002.

5. Gregg Vanourek, Bruno V. Manno, Chester E. Finn Jr., and Louann A. Bierlein, *Charter Schools in Action Project*, Hudson Institute, Part I: Table 4, June 1997.

6. Ibid., Part I: Table 5.

7. Isabel Lyman, *The Homeschooling Revolution* (Amherst, MA: Bench Press International, 2000), 32.

8. National Education Association, NEA 2001–2002 Resolutions, Section B-69.

9. Jon Dougherty, "Home-schoolers Outperform Peers," WorldNetDaily.com, 23 October 2001.

10. Lawrence M. Rudner, *Scholastic Achievement and Demographic Characteristics of Home School Students in 1998*, Education Policy Analysis Archives, 2, 23 March 1999.

11. Julie Foster, "Home-schoolers Score Highest on ACT," WorldNetDaily.com, 22 August 2000.

12. Letter from Bob Chase to Nicky Hardenbergh (National Home Education Network legislative director), 26 February 2002, posted on-line at www.nea.org/resolutions/00/00b-68.html.

13. Amy White, "Homework (Home Schooling)," *St. Louis Post-Dispatch*, 15 August 2002.

Chapter 6: Homosexual Wrongs

1. Dr. James Dobson, national daily radio broadcast, 21 March 2001.

2. Joyce Howard Price, "Scouts Lose United Way Funds Over Gay Ban," *Washington Times*, 15 March 2002.

3. Jeff Johnson, "Kennedy, Clinton Promote Homosexual 'Rights' Bill," CNSNews.com, 27 February 2002.

4. Ibid.

5. Press Release, Pacific Justice Institute, 4 April 2002.

6. National Education Association Resolutions, B-31, 2001–2002.

7. NEA Task Force on Sexual Orientation, "Report of the NEA Task Force on Sexual Orientation," Reference 4, 8 February 2002.

8. Celeste McGovern, "Homosexual Awareness for Kindergarten," *Report Newsmagazine*, 15 April 2002.

9. *O'Reilly Factor*, FOX News, 18 April 2002.

10. Claudine Chamberlain, "Where Did the 'Gay Gene' Go?" ABCNews.com, 22 April 1999.

11. Ibid.

12. George Rice et al., "Male Homosexuality: Absence of Linkage to Microsatellite Markers at Xq28," *Science*, 284 (1999), 665–67.

13. Ibid.

14. Dr. Warren Throckmorton, "Initial Empirical and Clinical Findings Concerning the Change Process for Ex-Gays," APA Journal *Professional Psychology: Research and Practice,* June 2002.

15. Kathryn Jean Lopez, "The Cookie Crumbles," *National Review,* 23 October 2000.

16. Bill Maier, "Homosexual 'Big Brothers'?" *Family News in Focus,* 15 July 2002.

17. Karla Jay and Allen Young, *The Gay Report: Lesbians and Gay Men Speak Out About Sexual Experiences and Lifestyle* (New York: Summit Books, 1979), 275.

18. Maier, "Homosexual 'Big Brothers'?"

19. Dr. Jeffrey Satinover, *Homosexuality and the Politics of Truth* (Grand Rapids, MI: Hamewith Books, 1996), 69.

20. *O'Reilly Factor,* FOX News, 7 September 2002.

Chapter 7: Abortion: The American Holocaust

1. Bryan A. Garner, "Abortion," in *Black's Law Dictionary,* 7th ed. (St. Paul, MN: West Group, 1999).

2. Benjamin Frank Miller and Thomas Eoyang, "Transfusion," in *Miller-Keane Encyclopedia & Dictionary of Medicine, Nursing, & Allied Health,* 6th ed. (Philadelphia: W. B. Saunders Co., 1997).

3. Andrew Sloane, "Singer, Preference Utilitarianism and Infanticide," in *Rethinking Peter Singer,* edited by Gordon Preece (Downers Grove, IL: InterVarsity Press, 2002), 68–94.

4. Stanley K. Henshaw, "Abortion Incidence and Services in the United States, 1995–1996," *Family Planning Perspectives,* November-December 1998.

5. "Abortion Techniques: Suction Aspiration," National Right to Life Web site, posted on-line at www.nrlc.org/abortion/ASMF/asmf4.html.

6. L. I. Remennick, "Induced Abortion As a Cancer Risk Factor: A Review of Epidemiological Evidence," *Journal of Epidemiological Community Health*, 1990; and M. C. Pike, "Oral Contraceptive Use and Early Abortion As Risk Factors for Breast Cancer in Young Women," *British Journal of Cancer*, 43 (1981), 72.

7. "Choosing Abortions: Questions and Answers: Page 3," Planned Parenthood Federation of America Web site, posted on-line at www.plannedparenthood.org/ABORTION/chooseabort3.html.

8. Elliot Institute, "A List of Major Psychological Sequelae of Abortion," posted on-line at www.afterabortion.org/psychol.html.

9. Mika Gissler, Elina Hemminki, and Jouko Lonnqvist, "Suicides After Pregnancy in Finland: 1987–94: Register Linkage Study," *British Medical Journal*, 313 (1996), 1431–34.

10. David Reardon, "Psychological Reactions Reported After Abortion," *The Post-Abortion Review*, fall 1994, 4–8.

11. Mika Gissler, "Pregnancy-Associated Deaths in Finland 1987-1994: Definition Problems and Benefits of Record Linkage," *Acta Obstetricia et Gynecologica Scandinavica*, 76 (1997), 651–57.

12. Remennick, "Induced Abortion As a Cancer Risk Factor," and Pike, "Oral Contraceptive Use and Early Abortion As Risk Factors for Breast Cancer in Young Women."

13. Dr. Janet Daling, "Risk of Breast Cancer Among Young Women: Relationship to Induced Abortion," 86th Journal of the National Cancer Institute, 1994.

14. "Choosing Abortions: Questions and Answers: Page 3," Planned Parenthood Federation of America Web site.

15. Phillip G. Stubblefield, M.D., "Pain of First-Trimester Abortion: Its Quantification and Relations with Other Variables," *American Journal of Obstetrics and Gynecology,* 133, no. 5 (1979), 489.

16. Nancy Wells, "Pain and Distress During Abortion," *Health Care for Women International,* 12 (1991), 296–97.

17. Eliane Bélanger, Ronald Melzak, and Pierre Lauzon, "Pain of First-Trimester Abortion: A Study of Psychosocial and Medical Predictors," *Pain,* 36 (1989), 343, 345.

18. Dinesh D'Souza, *Letters to a Young Conservative* (New York: Basic Books, 2002), 192.

19. Lisa Adams, "My Horror Find After Ordeal of Abortion," *Daily Record,* 8 October 2002.

20. Ramesh Ponnuru, "Not Dead Yet," *National Review,* 17 May 1999.

21. Remarks to the students and faculty, St. John's University, New York, New York, 28 March 1985.

Chapter 8: Big Daddy

1. Franklin Delano Roosevelt, "On the Reorganization of the Judiciary," 22, *Works of Franklin D. Roosevelt,* 9 March 1937.

2. Associated Press, "Bush Endorses Homeland Security Plan," 13 November 2002.

3. Jack Money, "City Studies Plan to Hook Bass Pro," *Daily Oklahoman,* 17 October 2001.

4. Associated Press, "Nearly Half of Americans Think First Amendment Goes Too Far, Survey Finds," 29 August 2002.

5. Edgar Simpson, "Everybody Can't Eat the Food," *Joplin Globe,* 25 February 2001.

6. Remarks by Ronald Reagan to representatives of the Future Farmers of America, 28 July 1988.

Chapter 9: Dividing the Line

1. David Barton, *Original Intent: The Courts, the Constitution and Religion* (Aledo, TX: Wallbuilder Press, 2002), 46.

2. David Barton, "The Myth of Church-State Separation," *Whistleblower*, 10, no. 12, published monthly by WorldNetDaily.com (Selma, OR), December 2001, 7.

3. Constitution of the state of Mississippi, Catherine Millard, *The Rewriting of America's History* (Camp Hill, PA: Horizon House, 1991), 390.

4. Constitution of the state of South Carolina, John J. McGrath, ed., *Church and State in American Law: Cases and Materials* (Milwaukee, WI: Bruce Publishing Company, 1962), 375.

5. Constitution of the state of Georgia, Benjamin Weiss, *God in American History: A Documentation of America's Religious Heritage* (Grand Rapids, MI: Zondervan, 1966), 155.

6. Americans United for Separation of Church and State, About Page, posted at www.au.org/about.htm.

7. Constitution of the state of Massachusetts, Weiss, *God in American History*, 155.

8. Barton, *Original Intent: The Courts, the Constitution, and Religion*, 143.

9. Constitution of the state of Connecticut, Gary DeMar, *God and Government* (Atlanta: American Vision, 1984), 164.

10. Barton, *Original Intent: The Courts, the Constitution, and Religion*, 155.

11. Peter Marshall and David Manuel, *From Sea to Shining Sea* (Old Tappan, NJ: Revell, 1986), 412.

12. Peter Marshall and David Manuel, *The Glory of America* (Bloomington, MN: Garborg's Heart'N Home, 1991), 12.

13. David Limbaugh, *Absolute Power* (Washington, DC: Regnery 2001), introduction, x.

14. Gary DeMar, *The Untold Story* (Atlanta: American Vision, 1993), 78, 121.

15. Tim LaHaye, *Faith of Our Founding Fathers* (Brentwood, TN: Wolgemuth and Hyatt, 1987), 192–93.

16. Associated Press, "ACLU Challenges Mayor's Ban of Satan in Florida," 23 January 2002.

17. David Limbaugh, "Yet More Assaults on Christianity," Creator's Syndicate, 2 February 2002.

18. LaHaye, *Faith of Our Founding Fathers*, 122–24.

Chapter 10: The Founders Again

1. David Limbaugh covers this in great detail in *Absolute Power.*

2. Ibid.

3. Thomas West, *Vindicating the Founders* (New York: Rowman and Littlefield, 1997), 39.

4. Millard, *The Rewriting of America's History,* 433–37.

5. Americanus [Timothy Ford], "The Constitutionalist," in *American Political Writing During the Founding Era, 1760–1805,* vol. 2, edited by Charles S. Hyneman and Donald S. Lutz (Indianapolis: Liberty Fund, 1983), 928–29.

6. Jess Bravin, "D.C. Cops Build Surveillance Network," *Wall Street Journal,* 13 February 2002.

7. Jennifer Brown, "Oklahoma City Victims Feel Slighted," Associated Press, 26 August 2002.

8. David Barton, *The Myth of Separation* (Aledo, TX: Wallbuilder Press, 1992), 113.

9. Alexander Fraser Tytler (Lord Woodhouseless), *The Decline and Fall of the Athenian Republic*, 1776.

10. Ibid.

Conclusion: Which Is the Greatest Generation?

1. Walter E. Williams, "The 'Great Generation'?" WorldNetDaily.com, 13 November 2002.

Appendix: Young Activists

1. David Yeagley, "Lone Leftist Kills Oklahoma Patriotism Bill," *Front Page*, 5 April 2002.

ACKNOWLEDGMENTS

When such a massive project is thrown my way, it's definitely not something you can pull off solo. It took a lot of hard work and determination, but I didn't do it by myself.

First and foremost, I'd like to thank God for giving me this ability to write, guiding me in what to do in this book, and guiding me in general throughout my life that is just beginning.

Joseph Farah, the founder of WorldNetDaily and partner in WND Books, for approaching me with this project—I know that the thought of investing in the writings of a young teenager is hard to sell, so I appreciate it.

My editor, Joel Miller, who is fantastic at what he does—I'd hate to have his job in editing my work. He also helped me get this idea jump-started, from the outline and proposal, to the end of the tedious work of editing.

I also want to thank all the folks over at WorldNetDaily for their encouragement and for accepting a kid who likes to ask questions.

Finally, I want to show my appreciation to my immediate and extended family for their encouragement and their willingness to put up with me—notably my grandmother for her prayers. Additionally, I'd like to thank all those here in our small town for their acceptance and encouragement—a group that is too big to list.

ACKNOWLEDGMENTS

I especially want to thank my parents:

My mom, Debbie Williams, who has been on my one-person staff since the beginning. She was tireless in her research and helping find the information I needed to complete the task. She encouraged me when I needed it, she took it easy on me, sometimes too much, but she helped me wrap it up in the home stretch when we were all tired. Thanks, Mom.

My dad, Don Williams, who did as best he could in keeping me on track and staying focused, but also gave me invaluable constructive criticism and helped me with the editing and flow of the book. As he is a much better writer than I, he helped me very much in my ideas and writing. Thanks, Dad.

ABOUT THE AUTHOR

KYLE WILLIAMS, A FOURTEEN-YEAR-OLD, WAS FIRST introduced to WorldNetDaily.com readers in 2001 as its newest columnist. His weekly column, *Veritas,* was an instant hit. Home-schooled in rural Oklahoma, Williams brings a fresh perspective to the debate table, shattering stereotypes about the apathy of youth. He is sharp, salient, and sure to upset the reigning liberal orthodoxy with perceptive criticisms. He possesses a driving desire to expose liberal propaganda in the nation's schools and media, and he encourages other young Americans to express their views, trusting that the truth—*veritas*—will win in the end. When not tackling tough political issues, Kyle likes to play baseball, football, and basketball. He also plays several instruments, including the guitar and piano, and Kyle is also very active in his church.

WND BOOKS

A Division of Thomas Nelson, Inc.

The pen is indeed mightier than the sword. In an age where swords are being rattled all over the world, a new voice has emerged. An unprecedented partnership between WorldNetDaily, the leading independent Internet news site, and Thomas Nelson, Inc., one of the leading publishers in America, has brought about a new book-publishing venture—WND Books.

You can find WND Books at your favorite bookstore or by visiting the Web sites www.WorldNetDaily.com or www.WNDBooks.com

CENTER OF THE STORM (ISBN 0-7852-6443-4)—Former Florida Secretary of State Katherine Harris discusses behind-the-scenes negotiations, backroom bartering, and the twelve essential principles that helped her not just survive but thrive during the infamous 2000 presidential election vote recount.

• • •

THE SAVAGE NATION (ISBN 0-7852-6353-5)—In this *New York Times* #1 bestseller, Michael Savage, host of the fourth largest radio talk show, uses bold, biting, and hilarious straight talk to take aim at the sacred cows of our ever-eroding culture and the "group of psychopaths" known as PETA, the ACLU, and the liberal media.

• • •

FIRST STRIKE (ISBN 0-7852-6354-3)—With an impressive array of facts, Jack Cashill and James Sanders show the relationship between the TWA Flight 800 disaster of July 1996 and the September 11 attacks in 2001 and proclaim how and why the American government has attempted to cover up the truth.

• • •

AT ANY PRICE (ISBN 0-7852-6365-9)—Patricia Roush's girls were kidnapped more than sixteen years ago and taken by their Saudi father to the kingdom of Saudi Arabia. In the midst of this tragic set of circumstances came an ongoing, demoralizing struggle with the U.S. government and the Saudi kingdom to reunite her with her children.

Praise for *Taking America Back*
(ISBN 0-7852-6392-6)

"Joseph Farah has written a thought-provoking recipe for reclaiming America's heritage of liberty and self-governance. I don't agree with all the solutions proposed here, but Farah definitely nails the problems."

—RUSH LIMBAUGH

"I don't agree with everything Joseph Farah says in *Taking America Back*, but he has written a provocative, from-the-heart call to action. It's a must-read for anyone who wonders how we can expand liberty and reclaim the vision of our founders."

—SEAN HANNITY

"Joseph Farah and I share a fierce passion for protecting children and a belief that without the Ten Commandments there would be no U.S. Constitution or Bill of Rights. Every American who shares our convictions should read this book."

—DR. LAURA C. SCHLESSINGER

• • •

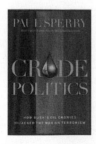

Available June 2003:
CRUDE POLITICS (ISBN 0-7852-6271-7)— WorldNetDaily.com's Washington bureau chief Paul Sperry presents alarming evidence that, true to America's foreign policy of the last century, the Bush administration seized the opportunity to use the September 11, 2001, attacks as reason to oust the Taliban—the major obstacle blocking plans for a gas and oil pipeline in Afghanistan.